Confessions of

EMERGENCY ROOM
DOCTORS

Confessions of

EMERGENCY ROOM
DOCTORS

Rocky Lang and Dr. Erick Montero

**Andrews McMeel
Publishing, LLC**

Kansas City

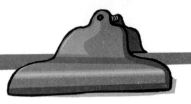

07 08 09 10 11 RR2 10 9 8 7 6 5 4 3 2 1

ISBN-13: 978-0-7407-6863-7
ISBN-10: 0-7407-6863-8

Library of Congress Control Number: 2007923205

www.andrewsmcmeel.com

www.confessionsofERDocs.com

ATTENTION: SCHOOLS AND BUSINESSES
Andrews McMeel books are available at quantity discounts with bulk
purchase for educational, business, or sales promotional use. For
information, please write to: Special Sales Department, Andrews McMeel
Publishing, LLC, 4520 Main Street, Kansas City, Missouri 64111.

To my wife, Heather, who keeps her
thirty-year-old tonsils
in a jar in our living room

—Rocky

To my daughter, Lara

—Erick (your papa)

The Patch

Sometimes you just want to laugh. There was a patient who came back to the hospital for a follow-up appointment and informed me that she was having trouble with one of her medications. "Which one?" I asked. "These patches. I was told to put on a new one every six hours and now I'm running out of places to put it!"

After disrobing her I discovered that the patient had taken the instructions literally and had placed over thirty patches on her body! She obviously didn't read the instructions that said to remove the old patch before applying a new one.

—Anonymous

I Sing the Body Electric

First of all, until we established a transportation department in Central, we had the key to the morgue and that was the start of my wits being scared out of me. Rumor used to be that I hid my beer in the body fridges to keep it cold, which I'm not going to confirm or deny, but that's another story.

One night, we got an eighty-one-year-old lady in full cardiac arrest. I happened to be there and we went to a full-court press, unfortunately to no avail. This lady died.

I took her to the morgue and continued about the rest of my shift. About an hour later, I got a page from Jane, my supervisor, asking me to meet her in the morgue. I jetted down there, and the whole code team was there, with the exception of Tim, one of the ER staff nurses. I should have known something was up, but it didn't quite register.

I was told that this poor lady's husband wanted to view her body one last time and would I please give the nurses a hand with the lifting.

"OK, why not?" I said and gloved up. The body was still on this yucky gurney, full of blood left over from trying to save her life, and there were holes in her body left by the tubes. The plan was to take her off the bloodstained gurney and put her on a nice one for her husband to see.

When I started to lift this body, which was damn heavy and seemed like the wrong one, I said, "Guys, this is the wrong patient." And at that very moment the body, shrouded in the white Hefty bag sat up and let out this low baritone moan. "WEAHAAA!" I jumped back and cocked my fist! I was ready to hit this dead body! I would have killed it if it weren't already dead. Anyway, the shroud falls off the head and I see this ghoulish face staring back at me. Damnit, if it wasn't Tim with a nasal canula hanging out of his nose. As soon as I recognized him I yelled, "Damn all of you!" I was shaking and quivering like Mike Tyson at a sixth-grade spelling bee!

Meanwhile, I hear Darcy, another nurse say, "Oh no!" I turned and saw that Jane had laughed her way into urinary incontinence. She flooded her undies right there in the morgue! I was not quick to offer her scrubs to finish her shift.

It was quite a group of people, lots of fun. They poured some Betadine solution around Tim's neck, wrapped him up in a body bag, threw an oxygen tank under the gurney, and snuck a tube up through the bag so he wouldn't suffocate. Yes, they got me!

All of the involved RNs have since migrated, but I'll never forget them.

—Dan the Man, Northridge, California
(He wanted to be called Dan the Man.
But otherwise, just call him Danny.)

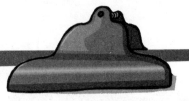

SEEN AND HEARD

✓ Overheard in the ER, a nurse consoled a hard-of-hearing family member. "No, Mrs. Margolin, not the HEARSE, I'm sending the NURSE!"

✓ A gynecological consultant from North Wales tells the story that while passing through a frantic ENT (ear, nose, and throat) clinic, he overheard this curious bit of conversation where an attending doctor angrily asked a nurse for his auriscope. She replied that she couldn't get it until he told her his star sign.

✓ Years ago, a former radiologist from Northern Ireland, dressed up in leaden apron and gloves, was X-raying a patient.

When her clothing caused some opacity on the fluorescent screen, he remarked, "Would you pull down your knickers, please?"

The patient did nothing so he repeated the request. He then heard her say, "I'm so sorry, doctor. I thought you were talking to the nurse."

MEDICAL RECORDS

By the time he was admitted, his rapid heart had stopped, and he was feeling better.

Patient has chest pain if she lies on her left side for over a year.

The patient states there is a burning pain in his penis, which goes to his feet.

On the second day the knee was better and on the third day it had completely disappeared.

The patient has been depressed ever since she began seeing me in 1983.

I will be happy to go into her GI system; she seems ready and anxious.

Weekend at Bernie's

or Always Wear Your Seatbelt

It was a while back before the regulations we have now. A guy died in the ER with no family to speak of. No one came to pick him up so we stuck him in the cooler until "Station Wagon Guy" came by to retrieve him. We called him this because he drove this wagon that had a refrigeration unit in it.

At one point it must have been used to transport meat and poultry. Otherwise, it was just a regular wagon that one would see anywhere—but this guy converted it to transport dead bodies. Station Wagon Guy went from one hospital to another picking up dead people who were unclaimed and taking them to the morgue.

So this night he stops by the ER and picks up the two bodies we have on ice. He opens up the back of the wagon and with the help of one of the orderlies, slides one of the bodies on top of a few others and closes the door. Then he realizes that there is one more stiff to transport and there is no more room in the wagon. We tell him we'll keep the guy on ice and he can come back. He says, "No way I'm coming back tonight."

He goes over to the wagon, opens the passenger side door, and then with a little help he bends the guy into a sitting position and slides him into the front seat, straps the seatbelt on him, says "good-night" to us, and drives away. It sort of reminded me of the movie *Weekend at Bernie's* except the guy was in a body bag.

—Anonymous

Barbeque and Corn

Why do people eat before getting stabbed? One of my favorites was when a guy came into the ER after being stabbed in the abdomen at a barbeque. He must have eaten in a hurry because he certainly didn't chew very well. When I looked at the wound, he coughed and his dinner came dripping out of his wound: Right in front of us was a complete Texas BBQ. We spent twenty minutes picking barbeque and corn out of the loops of his intestine after fixing the hole in his stomach.

—Dr. D.N.D., Texas

Smuckers

This was a pretty funny one. We get a lot of older people at the clinic and I'll never forget when this woman from Portugal came in complaining of a purple discharge from her vagina. She thought it might have something to do with the diaphragm that her doctor had recently given her. "I read the instructions on the packet and I used it with the jelly." When the nurse asked her which kind of jelly she had used, she told us . . . "Grape."

—Anonymous

Traffic

"It was about 10:30 P.M. when a ninety-five-year-old woman came into the ER in full cardiac arrest. We worked on her for about thirty minutes trying to resuscitate her, but soon it was obvious there was nothing else we could do, and she was pronounced dead. It is always difficult telling a family member that a loved one has died, and when I went into the waiting room, I was face-to-face with the woman's seventy-two-year-old daughter. I told her, "I'm sorry, your mother didn't make it." The lady blinked and said, "Didn't make it? The traffic must have been horrible, she left with the ambulance over an hour ago."

—Anonymous

The following answers are purported to come from premed students from around the world. They have been compiled from several sources.

GENERAL:

"The body consists of three parts—the brainium, the borax, and the abominable cavity. The brainium contains the brain; the borax, the heart and lungs; and the abominable cavity, the bowel, of which there are five—a, e, i, o, and u."

RESPIRATION:

"When you breathe, you inspire. When you do not breathe, you expire."

"Respiration consists of two acts: first inspiration, then expectoration."

CARDIOVASCULAR:

"The three kinds of blood vessels are arteries, veins, and caterpillars."

GASTROINTESTINAL:

"The alimentary canal is located in the northern part of Alabama."

DENTISTRY:

"A permanent set of teeth consists of eight canines, eight cuspids, two molars, and eight cuspidors."

ORTHOPEDICS:

"The skeleton is what is left after the insides have been taken out and the outsides have been taken off. The purpose of the skeleton is something to hitch meat on."

REPRODUCTIVE MEDICINE:

"Artificial insemination is when the farmer does it to the cow instead of the bull."

"To prevent contraception, wear a condominium."

HEMATOLOGY:

"Before giving a blood transfusion, find out if the blood is affirmative or negative."

EAR, NOSE, AND THROAT:

"To remove dust from the eye: Pull the eye down over the nose to top of throat."

"For nosebleeds, put the nose lower than the body until the heart stops."

Frankenstein

We had a patient that was brain dead and our team decided to approach the family about organ-procurement. We knew that our patient had at least six organs that could help save the lives of others and it was my job to ask them if it would be OK.

I approached the family that was gathered around the patient's bed and posed the question. There was an immediate response of enthusiasm. The wife said, "Yes! Most definitely we would agree to a brain transplant."

She must not have understood me, I thought. I said to her, "No, we are not yet medically capable of implanting brains and besides if we were, your husband wouldn't have the soul, memory, or any characteristics of the person you know."

She didn't seem to mind and said that was OK and she still wanted a brain transplant and had seen dozens of movies including *Frankenstein* where a brain was transplanted from one person to the other.

When I finally got through to her that it was not possible and what we wanted to do was to take her husband's organs to implant into other patients in need, the family said no. It's always been something that bothered me that a family is willing to take an organ, but is not willing to give one.

—Anonymous

Farmer John

This guy had so many DUIs they took away his driver's license but that was not going to deter him. He got smashed one night, and decided to ride his lawn mower down the interstate to a liquor store to get a six-pack. The problem was he was driving down the middle of the highway when a semi coming the wrong way hit him—and then we had to put him back together.

—Dr. D.N.D, Texas

Plica Polnica

A disease primarily found in Poland where the skin and nails turn spongy and black. Hair emits a horrible odor, exudes a gluey liquid, and is painful to the touch.

Belly Button

I saw a lot of things in the emergency room and in my private practice, but I guess the most ridiculous thing was when a twenty-seven-year-old male came in at 2:00 A.M. with a complaint of lint in his belly button.

—Anonymous

Taxi Please!

It was early morning and things were pretty slow as the ER goes until a man raced in and yelled, "My girlfriend's going to have my kid in the taxi!" I grabbed my equipment, busting through doors. I remember it was very cold outside and jumped into the cab. I lifted the lady's dress, and began to take off her underwear. Suddenly I noticed that there were several cabs in line, and I had picked the wrong one.

—Anonymous

Double D's

Sometimes you get a patient that is older and hard of hearing. A woman came in to the ER complaining of shortness of breath. I placed a stethoscope on her chest and asked her to give me some big breaths. She smiled at me and said, "Oh young man, at one time they were big breasts."

—Anonymous

Passing by Gas

One day during my residency in Atlanta, I had to tell a husband that there was nothing left for us to do to his wife. She had died of a massive myocardial infarct, otherwise known as a heart attack. His sister came to join him and asked what had happened. He shook his head and said, "The doctor said that Margie died of a massive fart."

—Anonymous

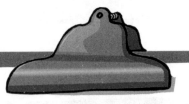

THE X IN Rx

There seems to be three explanations for the x in Rx,
the symbol for prescription.

1. Originally it was an astrological sign for the planet
   Jupiter and originated in the Middle Ages, when doctors
   believed that the planets influenced health. Jupiter, the
   largest planet, was thought to be the most powerful of
   all the heavenly bodies in curing disease. In old medieval
   manuscripts, all of the R's were crossed so the Rx symbol
   was a sign of corruption or the ancient symbol of the Roman
   god Jupiter. Those who are interested in astrology will know
   the symbol, which has a crossed leg at the bottom right.

2. Some maintain that the Rx is an abbreviation for "recipe."
   In the early days pharmacists, who were also doctors, mixed
   various medicines in their apothecaries—and in a way, they
   were cooking up a recipe.

3. The original pharmaceutical symbol was an eye with an
   "x" below it instead of the "R" and was called "The Eye of
   Horus," who was the father of pharmacy. This was a very
   powerful symbol in ancient Egypt and it was worn to ensure
   good health and ward off sickness. It looks like an Rx.

The X's in Medicine

Dx = diagnoses

Fx = fracture

Hx = history

Rx = prescriptions

Sx = symptoms

Tx = treatment or transplant

The Jolly Green Giant

Well, for me, the vine in the vagina comes to mind. A little old lady who I thought was demented came into the ER with the chief complaint of, "I have the vine in the vagina."

I was working for a county teaching hospital and decided to play a little joke on one of the new residents. He was a very conservative private-sector kind of guy who was having a hard time. I didn't really look at the lady's vagina but got her undressed and told the resident that he had to see her "RIGHT AWAY!" I had the sheet over her legs and when he went to push them apart to do the pelvic exam, out pops the vine. The Jolly Green Giant was right there.

We were rather surprised. He pushed back on the stool, hit the wall, almost falling off and knocking the X-ray viewer off the wall. This caused such a racket that people came running into the exam room and of course screamed when they saw her. Needless to say, we both looked like idiots. The lady had put a piece of potato in her vagina to hold up a prolapsed uterus and forgot to take it out.

—Tonya, RN, San Francisco, California

Brown Bagging It

I had been up nearly eighteen hours and the air conditioning was going off and on. It was August, and it was damn hot. I couldn't wait to get home. Anyway, I was told that a patient had just been admitted with severe abdominal pains and was in Room 3. I entered the examination room and saw a woman in her mid-fifties, weighing at least three hundred pounds.

As I started to examine her, the smell was horrific. I didn't know where it was coming from but I noticed a brown piece of paper protruding from under her left breast. I asked her what it was and she laughed and lifted her breast revealing a brown paper bag. She told me that in the past she had a tendency to leave her lunch on the bus, so, starting about a year ago, she would make her lunch and tuck it under her breast so she wouldn't forget it.

—Dr. Todd, Atlanta, Georgia

Bedridden

Older patients often say very funny things and it's hard not to laugh. One patient came into the ER from a nursing home and while checking her out I asked, "How long have you been bedridden?" She laughed at me and said, "Oh doctor, don't flatter me, it's been a very long time since I did anything like that."

—Dr. Hal, Los Angeles, California

Blue Grass of Kentucky

There was an older woman, I think her name was Doris, who I was caring for while doing my residency in Kentucky. I came by one morning and asked, "So how was your breakfast this morning?"

"It was very good," she said, smiling. "Except for that there Kentucky jelly. I can't seem to get used to the taste."

I looked down at her tray and saw that the jelly she had put on her toast was labeled "KY Jelly."

—Anonymous

STRANGE NAMES FOR
DOCTORS

Dr. Dick Woodcock

———

Dr. Hart Achin

———

Drs. French and Fry

———

Dr. Wu Woo

———

Dr. Dick Dick

———

Dr. Fang, DDS

———

Dr. Khan Do

———

Dr. and Dr. Doctor *(married couple)*

———

Dr. Dekay

———

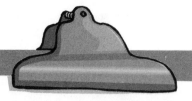

MEDICAL FACTS

✓ Surgical teams accidentally leave clamps, sponges, and other tools inside about 1,500 patients nationwide each year.

✓ Men are twice as likely to contract leprosy as women.

✓ It has been stated that a human can not catch a cold or the flu while at the North Pole. The winter temperatures are so low that none of the standard disease-causing microorganisms can survive.

Hot Dogs

We were doing a new obstetrics rotation and there was a young doctor who was clearly uncomfortable with examining women. I thought OB/GYN was definitely a field he wasn't going to pursue. Anyway, it was time for him to examine a beautiful twenty-five-year-old woman and he began to whistle quietly. It only took a second before the woman started laughing. When we realized what the song was, we started laughing as well. He looked up over his glasses and asked, "Is there something wrong?" We all looked at each other when the patient said, "No, nothing's the matter, you're only whistling 'I want to be a Oscar Mayer Wiener.'"

—Anonymous

Recycle

This guy comes into the ER and said he was trying to commit suicide by swallowing five teaspoons of bottle caps. He was going to go for seven, but he had had enough, besides . . . chopping them up into smaller pieces was proving difficult. We called him the "Ostrich Man" and he was a regular in the ER. We had seen him before with a stomach full of pieces of string or plastic, but the bottle caps were a new thing.

—Anonymous

Revenge

A thirty-year-old nurse at a regional hospital had a bone to pick with her former lover and set out on getting revenge. She filled out papers stating that her ex-boyfriend was mentally unstable and committed him to the psychiatric ward. Police showed up to arrest the former paramour and it was only after hours of psychological evaluation that the doctors discovered he was quite sane and she might be the one who was crazy. Lynch was arrested and held on $5,000 bail.

—Various news sources

Jerry Springer Time

The strangest thing I ever saw in the ER was on a hot September night. Things were sort of slow when suddenly all hell broke loose. We knew from paramedics over the radio that we had two gunshot victims coming in. BAM, the doors opened and the first guy came in screaming at the top of his lungs. I'm telling you every expletive imaginable was coming out of this guy. He wouldn't stay down. We put him in triage number one and started working on him. It didn't seem like such a bad wound and we started running an IV. Then the second gunshot victim comes in. This guy is screaming louder than the first. We take a look at him, and his wound is also pretty superficial. So, we put him in triage number two. Then all of a sudden the guy in the first room hears who's in the other room and comes busting though the curtain. Then he pulls the guy off the gurney and they tumble into the hall falling over an X-ray machine. Now both of these guys have IVs hanging out of their arms and are still bleeding from their wounds. They are yelling at each other, cursing about their "mamas" and who's the "baddest dude." Turns out the guys were in separate gangs and were responsible for shooting each other. It was weird.

—Dr. Herb, Los Angeles, California

MEDICAL RECORDS

Patient was released to outpatient department without dressing. I have suggested that he loosen his pants before standing, and then, when he stands with the help of his wife, they should fall to the floor.

The patient is tearful and crying constantly. She also appears to be depressed.

Discharge status: Alive but without permission. The patient will need disposition, and therefore we will get Dr. Black to dispose of him.

Healthy, appearing decrepit, sixty-nine-year-old male, mentally alert but forgetful.

The patient has no past history of suicides.

NEWS AROUND THE WORLD

ENGLAND—A surgeon who amputated healthy limbs of two psychologically disturbed men said both men were delighted and making a rapid and satisfactory recovery.

PHILADELPHIA, PENNSYLVANIA—Twenty-five-year-old Blake Steidler of Reamstown mailed a bomb addressed to a doctor in Chicago. Steidler was angry with the doctor after a penis enlargement surgery was botched, and was later sentenced to four years and ten months in prison.

MEDINA, OHIO—A former nurse's aide was sentenced to ten months in prison for giving elderly patients large doses of milk of magnesia. The plan was to get back at a nurse coming on the next shift who would have to take care of the soon-to-be mess.

DELAWARE, OHIO—A man walked into a Delaware hospital emergency room and handed a clerk a note stating he wanted to donate his organs. After the clerk accepted the donor card, the man shot himself in the head.

—*News sources and Internet sites*

MUNCIE, INDIANA—In 2005, a January ice storm kept thousands in the dark and without heat for days. Nine months later there was a baby boom where more than twice the usual number of babies were born.

—*Various news sources*

No Smoking Please

A woman came into the ER, ready to give birth, followed by her husband and about ten kids.

Their last name was King. We took her to the OR (operating room) and soon I came out and announced that Mr. King was the proud father of a baby boy—I told him his wife said that he should name the little one. Mr. King scratched his head and said, "Gee I just don't know, I've just about used up all the names I can think of. He glanced up at a sign that read "NO SMOKING." "That's it" he said, "I'll name him Nosmo—Nosmo King."

—Dr. Harold, Los Angeles, California

Pencil Wit

A patient came running hysterically into the ER, "Help, Help!
I stabbed myself in the hand with a pencil—I'm going to die!" I
looked at his hand and saw that the pencil didn't even break the
skin. I told the man, "You're OK—you're not going to die." "No
doc, you don't understand," he said, showing me the pencil, "I'm
allergic to penicillin."

—Dr. Stewarts, Los Angeles, California

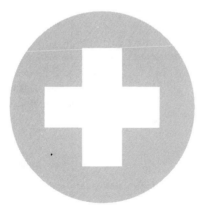

NEWS AROUND THE WORLD

HAILEY, IDAHO—An ambulance brought a woman to the ER who had over twenty cat bites, scratches, and puncture wounds on her body and face. A black-and-white domestic tomcat had gone completely berserk when a neighbor showed up with a different cat. The woman, who was in her sixties, said when she gets out of the hospital she will give the cat away.

KANSAS CITY, MISSOURI—Doctors reported that Melinda Abell was admitted to the emergency room with a cell phone lodged so deeply in her throat that they concluded her boyfriend must have forced it there.

Prosecutors say twenty-four-year-old Marlon Brando Gill was angry and jealous when he forced the phone into his girlfriend's throat. However, defense attorneys insist the twenty-five-year-old victim swallowed the phone intentionally to prevent Gill from finding out who she'd been calling.

A doctor at a Kansas City hospital's emergency room used a tool called a "pincher" to remove the phone from Abell's throat.

Gill was charged with felony first-degree assault and has recently been convicted of second-degree assault.

—*From various news sources*

NEW ORLEANS, LOUISIANA—A medical study stated that men delay medical care when a game is on. The study went on to say that there is a 40 percent drop in emergency room visits during a major game.

The Truth About Medicine

"I have an earache."

2000 B.C.—Eat this herb.

A.D. 1000—That herb is from the devil. Please chant.

A.D. 1750—Chanting is from the devil. Drink this potion.

A.D. 1930—That potion is snake oil. Here, take this pill.

A.D. 1980—That pill is ineffective. Here, take this antibiotic.

A.D. 2000—That antibiotic has chemicals in it. Here, eat this herb.

—As passed on from doctor to doctor

'Nother Beer Please

An inebriated man staggered into the ER complaining of severe pain while trying to remove his contact lenses. He claimed that he was only able to get them half out but they always popped back in. A nurse tried to help using a suction pump, but without success. Finally, a doctor examined him and discovered the man did not have his contact lenses in at all. He had been trying to rip out the membrane of his cornea.

—Dr. M., Oakland, California

Another One Flew Over
the Cuckoo's Nest

I'm working in the psych ward when a call came in on a guy who had been admitted with chest pain. Now usually when they call in the shrink, who is me, it's some guy with psychosomatic issues. So I go down to see this guy flat out on the bed, EKG beeping, tubes coming out of him and of course . . . he's a moaner. He points to his chest, "Deep pressure pains . . . ohhhh, hurts, ohhhh." So I ask, "You think you're having a heart attack?" The guy says, "Oh no. . . . I've got seven lesbians in my heart and when they put their arms out to the side it really hurts. They do that when they are mad at me." Now, I've seen a lot in my years but I had never heard this one. So I ask the guy, "How did the seven lesbians get into your heart?" He looked up at me, his eyes welling up with tears, "I'm afraid of turning gay, so I put the lesbians there to protect me."

—Dr. G, Baltimore, Maryland

NEWS AROUND THE WORLD

PORT ARTHUR, TEXAS—A young man appeared in the emergency room with bruises and two black eyes. A 9 mm bullet was lodged just under the skin in the middle of his forehead. Police wanted the bullet back, but the patient refused.

Prosecutors said that the retrieval of the bullet would prove that the patient, a seventeen-year-old gang member, had tried to kill the owner of a used-car lot after a robbery and that they had a search warrant to extract the slug. However, the patient's lawyers and doctors refused, stating privacy issues. Doctors are caught between wanting to help solve the crime and their responsibility to the patient's rights to refuse a procedure.

SEATTLE, WASHINGTON—Seattle police launched an investigation to determine how a patient undergoing emergency heart surgery caught on fire at a local hospital in 2003.

The male patient, who was not identified, went up in flames after alcohol that was poured on his skin was ignited by a surgical instrument.

The patient died after the surgery, but that was due to heart failure and not the fire. Although fires in operating rooms are extremely rare, they do happen.

—*Various news sources*

MANCHESTER, ENGLAND—A London ambulance crew was sent two hundred miles in the wrong direction to Manchester by a faulty satellite navigation system while transporting a patient to a hospital.

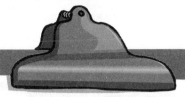

INJURY FACTS

✓ According to the National Electronic Injury Surveillance System, 125,312 people are injured each year while in or around a bed.

THE STRANGEST INJURY OF ALL TIME

✓ Arguably, the strangest head injury of all time was sustained by Phineas P. Gage on September 13, 1848, and is known in medical history as the "American Crowbar Case."

Gage, who was twenty-five and the foreman on the Rutland Burlington Railroad, was setting a blast of dynamite. The blast went off prematurely driving a three-foot-long, thirteen-pound tamping iron completely through the left side of his face and out the back of his head. After a short time, Gage got up, was examined by doctors, and returned to his job. Years later after Gage died, the iron bar, along with a cast of his head, was placed in the museum of the Massachusetts Medical College.

Gentlemen, Start Your Engines

A twenty-eight-year old male was brought into the ER after an attempted suicide. The man had swallowed several nitroglycerin pills and a bottle of gin. When asked about the bruises on his head and chest, he said that they were because he rammed himself into the wall in an attempt to make the nitroglycerin explode.

—Anonymous

Melcryptovestimentaphiliac
A disease where someone compulsively steals ladies' underwear.

Your Wife May Be Hazardous to Your Health

In Istanbul, a man was admitted to the ER with broken legs, a fractured pelvis, and severe burns to his genitals.

As the story is told, his wife tried to kill a cockroach first by stamping on it, then by trying to flush it down the toilet, and then spraying it with a bug spray while it floated in the bowl.

Her husband had to urinate and dropped his cigarette butt into the toilet. The fumes ignited, causing a fireball to erupt from the toilet that caused the burns on his genitals.

Paramedics were summoned, and while transporting him, dropped him down the stairs breaking his legs and pelvis.

—Anonymous

Interns Know Better

This is not really an ER story but it comes to mind as I think back over the strange experiences I have had as a physician.

As the first month of internship wore on for me, things gradually became more organized and I slowly developed the ability to cope with my job. One good thing is that an intern really becomes familiar with his patients. I would realize in later years that I would never know my patients as well as I knew them during my internship. With a particularly sick patient, I might be in and out of their room two or three dozen times during the day. My mind was constantly crammed full of facts about each patient and occupied with the problems of their diagnosis and treatment.

Even the residents, who knew their patients quite well, did not have all the intimate details in mind as well as the interns. This fact was demonstrated dramatically one day on my service. Mr. Carson, a patient with kidney disease and kidney failure, had slowly gone sour. As the patient's condition deteriorated, I became a more frequent visitor to his room. I tried everything I could think of to alter the progress of the disease, but there was really not much left to do.

Inexorably, Mr. Carson's disease worsened. His breathing became more labored and it was only slightly improved by oxygen. Slowly, he lapsed into a coma. His family was always around and was very appreciative of the time I spent with them.

Due to the difficulty the patient had in breathing, I had experimented with different positions and found that Mr. Carson could breathe best when sitting almost upright. Thus, I had had the back of his bed cranked up, and the patient supported by pillows, so that he was half reclining, half sitting. (These were in the days when a crank moved the bed up and down.)

One morning I was on rounds with the resident, Dr. Harmes, who was also my boss, "Why do you have Mr. Carson propped up like that?" he asked.

I said, "He breathes better that way."

Dr. Harmes laughed, "Come on, now. He looks so uncomfortable. I think he'd be better lying down."

I said, "I don't know, Charlie. He doesn't breathe too well lying down."

This discourse had taken place at the patient's bedside in full hearing of several members of the family. By this point in his disease the patient's breathing was labored and noisy and when Dr. Harmes began to crank down the bed and it reached a position of being level, the loud breathing suddenly stopped. The family looked alarmed. Dr. Harmes frantically began to crank the bed up again, but when the bed reached its original upright position, Mr. Carson's breathing did not resume. I placed my stethoscope on the patient's chest and heard nothing. Efforts at external respiratory and cardiac resuscitation were futile.

I turned to the family and said, "I'm sorry, but he's dead."

The alarm on the faces of the women in the room quickly turned to grief and they began to sob. One of the men turned to Dr. Harmes and me and asked, "Did cranking down the bed kill him?" Dr. Harmes's face was pink. He said in an embarrassed voice, "Oh no, I don't think so. As you know, he was going to die pretty soon, anyway."

This episode was a convincing demonstration to me that my familiarity with my patients was a strong advantage in determining the appropriate care for them.

—**Dr. George, Ann Arbor, Michigan**

Pee Brain

A young woman brought her child into Children's Hospital for a routine check-up. When the nurse saw that the child's first name was listed as Urine, she wanted to know why this woman would name her child this.

The woman explained, "Well, my baby was born premature and had to stay in the ICU. She was very sick and they didn't know if she would make it. I couldn't decide what to name her, but the nurses said they would pray for her. One day I came in and the nurses had already named her. There was this paper on her incubator that said 'Please save Urine,' so I knew that they had named my baby."

—Anonymous

STRANGE NAMES FOR
DOCTORS

DR. RON SLAUGHTER *(surgeon)*

———

DR. LOOK *(ophthalmologist)*

———

DR. HURT *(pediatrician–ouch)*

———

DR. FLASH GORDON

———

DR. JOHN LOONEY *(psychiatrist)*

———

DRS. FRANK SINATRA AND DANNY THOMAS
(shared an office)

———

DRS. TONGUE AND GUMS *(shared an office)*

———

DR. JAMES D. CURE

———

DR. ALDEN COCKBURN *(urologist)*

———

NEWS AROUND THE WORLD

HARTLAND, MAINE—A twenty-three-year-old man was admitted to the ER with a hole in his hand. The man had apparently tried to commit suicide by crucifying himself on a homemade cross.

The man nailed one hand to the cross and then got stuck. Realizing that he couldn't nail the other hand by himself, he called 911.

—*Various news sources*

MOSCOW—A woman was treated and released from a Moscow hospital after a rotted floor gave way, crashing her and her bathtub into the apartment below.

She had been relaxing in the bath when the floor gave way, collapsing under the weight of the bathtub. Her downstairs neighbors immediately called an ambulance and the woman was treated at a local hospital for injuries to her leg but was otherwise unhurt.

—*European news sources*

LONDON—from the European Association of Urology.

Surgeons in China performed the first successful penis transplant. It was never explained how the man lost the organ but nevertheless, doctors did find a donor and attached it successfully.

The transplant was reversed two weeks later. Without elaborating, doctors said, "because of severe psychological problems of the recipient and his wife, the transplanted penis regretfully had to be cut off."

—*Various news sources*

Excedrin Headache #000

A man with a history of migraine headaches and drug- seeking behavior had already spent several hours in the ER waiting to be seen. Once he was placed in a room, the ER doctor told him he would not give him any narcotics, but was willing to try non-opiates to treat his migraine. The patient left the hospital very upset, then went outside to a nearby phone booth. He then used a pen and ripped his left eyeball out and called 911 from the phone booth. Once he got to the trauma room, he was given the desired dose of narcotics.

—Sally, RN, Oakland, California

An Eye for an Eye

A regular drunk in the neighborhood used to come into the ER
and pop out his glass eye and ask people to clean it up for him. He
always seemed to ask people who had not seen this before and the
phrase "Oh, shit!" was heard often.

—Sally, RN, Oakland, California

We Might Lose Her

During an exam on a very large man—by a small petite female physician—someone yelled, "Grab her ankles . . . we might lose her," when she got ready to do the rectal exams. Even the other patients started laughing.

—Dr. M, Alameda, California

The Old Fart

When I was young, I did some things I would get fired for today. There was a real uptight doctor, a real piece of work—maybe the vilest person I ever met. Anyway, I slipped a remote fart machine into his coat pocket. Every time he would talk to a patient, I would press the button. He tried to keep a straight face and kept talking to the patient. After a few really good ones, the patient finally said, "Really, doctor, this can wait if you need to go to the bathroom." The doctor denied that he had any "gas" problem. The patient didn't believe him and we fell apart laughing. After that, I lost my fart machine, but I'll tell you . . . there are some more docs who deserve the experience.

—Tina, RN, San Francisco, California

The following answers are purported to come from premed students from around the world. They have been compiled from several sources.

For a cold: Use an agoniser to spray the nose until it drops in your throat.

FIRST AID:

For fainting: Rub the person's chest or, if a lady, rub her arm above the head instead. Or, put the head between the knees of the nearest doctor.

For asphyxiation: Apply artificial respiration until the patient is dead.

For drowning: Climb on top of the person and move up and down to make artificial perspiration.

For dog bite: Put the dog away for several days. If he has not recovered, then kill him.

Did They Really Say That?
MEDICAL RECORDS

The patient expired on the floor uneventfully.

Patient has left his white blood cells at another hospital.

Patient was becoming more demented with urinary frequency.

The patient's past medical history has been remarkably insignificant with only a forty-pound weight gain in the past three days.

She slipped on the ice and apparently her legs went in separate directions in early December.

The patient left the hospital feeling much better except for her original complaints.

She has had no rigors or shaking chills, but her husband states she was very hot in bed last night.

Beam Me Up, Scotty

This one is really old—from the seventies. It could never happen now. We had this mobile CAT scan unit that would go into the community to help diagnose the underserved and transport people back to the ER.

There was this really funny radiologist, and when things were slow he would pick up winos from street corners. In an effort to encourage them to seek help for their drinking, he would place the patient on the table staring straight up at this futuristic scanning unit that was really a CAT scan. Then he'd disappear behind a drape and reemerge with a scary alien mask looking like he came out of a 1950s horror film. He'd stand over the wino, and tell them that aliens had abducted them as a study on alcoholics. Then he'd tell them sternly that if they didn't seek help soon, the next time they would be transported by the scan to a distant planet for further study.

—Dr. Tee, Oakland, California

Is This Really
in My Job Requirement?

It was in the old ER and I had this guy with AIDS and schizophrenia. He had diarrhea and was totally uncooperative and wouldn't even let me near the bed. In those days we kept a paper chart by the bed. Well, this guy was getting really combative, so I left the room to get some help. I came back with the sheriff and a sedative called Droperiodl to find him standing on the center of the gurney. He was covered in diarrhea and was towering over me. Somehow he had gotten the MD chart, and as I arrived he was wiping his ass with it. Then he threw it at the shelves in a grand flamboyant gesture. The diarrhea flung all over the shelves and it was horrible, but all I could do was laugh until we got him medicated and then I had to clean it up. It was a mess.

—Tina, RN, Oakland, California

But, It Hurts

A guy comes into the ER complaining of pain. "It's everywhere, doc." He pushes his side, "It hurts when I press here." Then he pushes down on his leg. "It hurts here too." Now, I'm watching him and how he presses his arm. "It hurts here." I looked at him and said, "Hey dude, your finger is broken."

—Anonymous

Tired Guy

A thirty-year-old male was brought into the ER because he tried to kill himself by taking an entire bottle of sleeping pills. We pumped his stomach, and left him in the room. When I came back to check on him, he asked, "Do you think you could get me some sleeping pills because I can't sleep."

—Anonymous

Just a Trim Please

To keep things sort of light when dealing with tough stuff all day, we often found a way of injecting a little humor into our day. One example is when a guy came into the ER who cut off his penis because it had "offended him." Like the Bible says, if your eye offend thee . . . pluck it out. Well, we sewed it back on. The funny part is that his last name was Morehead. We of course referred to him as patient Nohead.

—Nancy, RN, Los Angeles, California

Tastes Great—
Less Filling

In a distant land, during a distant time, a patient was hurriedly wheeled into the critical area of our emergency room. The nurse was yelling, "ARREST! CARDIAC ARREST!" As I began to initiate external cardiac compressions, one of my coresidents slapped me on the shoulder.

"What are you doing? That's Smith. He's faking. He's done this about three times in the last month." The other resident nudged me aside and sat the patient up, all the time yelling at him, "Smith, Smith, enough of this crap! Get out of here!"

Sure enough, Mr. Smith, a twenty-fiveish young man, opened his eyes and sheepishly responded, "Sorry, Doc." That's all, just "Sorry, Doc." He slid off the gurney and paced out of the area. However, it didn't end there.

About two weeks later, my coresident and I were again on during the graveyard shift. Same scenario. But this time, the nurses and doctors had decided on a different strategy. The nurses did not rush Mr. Smith down the hall. Rather, they slowly walked the gurney into the critical area stating, "I think Mr. Smith finally did it this time. He is as dead as can be."

"OK, then. Let's move him into the morgue," one of the other residents said.

Mr. Smith lied still as his clothes were removed and he was covered only by a bed sheet. Everyone had their mouths covered to avoid blowing the charade with a torrent of giggles. The gurney was stealthily wheeled into the nurses' break room, near a closed door. Everyone stood in the back of the darkened room waiting to see what Mr. Smith would do. After a few minutes, Mr. Smith crawled off the gurney, apparently not noticing the crew of professionals silently snickering behind him.

Smith gently rapped on the door, "Hello, hello out there. I'm not really dead."

Only a few seconds passed before Smith opened the door to his private morgue and, the white sheet scantily covering his body, jogged out of the emergency room, never to be seen again . . . we thought.

A few weeks later, the scene repeated itself, with a twist.

As background, many years ago there was a test performed by physicians at a patient's bedside to determine the state of heart failure. A bile salt, normally found in the body, was rapidly infused into a patient's large vein in the antecubital fossa. It was a very bitter-tasting substance. It is well known that the circulation time for blood to reach the base of the tongue (location of taste buds) from the antecubital fossa is twelve seconds. If a patient had significant heart failure the circulation time was delayed, perhaps to thirty seconds or even longer. The physician would time how long it took for the patient to taste something very bitter. If the patient had normal circulation as quickly as he/she tasted the bitter bile salt, the taste would pass. A watch with a second hand was used to time until tasting.

While patient Smith lay "dying," an intravenous line was inserted and the very same bile salt was hung, not for a short and rapid infusion, but as a constant drip. After thirty seconds of the constant infusion, he sat bolt upright, pulled out the intravenous line, and scampered out of the emergency room—truly never to be seen again.

After a suitable period of guffawing, there was an ever so brief moment when my coresident and I looked at each other with sober eyes and asked ourselves what we had become in the doomsday environment of a chaotic urban emergency room.

—Anonymous

NEWS AROUND THE WORLD

NEW BRUNSWICK, NEW JERSEY—A doctor who graduated from a New Jersey medical school and now practices in Los Angeles pleaded guilty to stealing a hand from a school cadaver and giving it to an exotic dancer.

The dancer kept the hand in a jar of formaldehyde in her bedroom in South Plainfield. She called the hand "Freddy." The case is pending while the doctor is free on $1,000 bail. The stripper was charged with receiving stolen property.

KENOSHA, WISCONSIN—A man was treated and released after getting trapped waist-deep in a vat of 100-degree viscous hot chocolate. The employee of Debelis Corporation was pushing chocolate down into a vat because it was stuck. As it became loose, he slid into the hopper.

Firefighters, police, and coworkers were not able to free him until the chocolate was thinned with cocoa butter. The patient suffered only minor injuries and was released.

—*Various news sources*

MIAMI, FLORIDA—Using a piece of Gore-Tex to make repairs, doctors performed corrective surgery on a baby born with his heart outside his chest.

The baby was having hiccups and when doctors performed an ultrasound, they saw that the heart was on the outside of the chest wall but pumping blood through the artery that was snaking back into the chest. Doctors had to open the chest, wrap the heart in Gore-Tex substituting it for the child's own pericardium, and then replace the heart on the inside.

SEATTLE, WASHINGTON—A fifty-four-year-old cancer patient sued the Swedish Medical Center in 2004 for allegedly setting her face and head on fire during biopsy surgery.

The patient awoke from anesthesia during the operation to discover her head on fire.

In a written statement, the hospital acknowledged that the patient had suffered burns to the back of her neck and scalp, adding that they were "perhaps due to the inadvertent ignition of an alcohol-based hair-styling product. The burn was treated immediately and appropriately."

—*Various news sources*

DENMARK—A patient undergoing an operation to remove a mole on his buttocks broke wind, causing a fire in the operating room and setting his genitals on fire.

The surgeon was removing a mole with an electric knife when the man broke wind, igniting a spark. His genitals had been washed with surgical alcohol and just caught fire. He's suing the hospital for pain and suffering and loss of income.

He says he had to take extra time off work and can't have sex with his wife.

—*Various news sources*

MONTREAL, CANADA—A sixty-five-year-old man became the first Canadian to live without a pulse. On November 23, 2006, Dr. Renzo Cecere implanted the "Heartmate II" mechanical heart into Gerard Langevin. The new mechanical heart is powered by batteries located in pouches on the body providing a constant flow of blood. Because of that, the patient has no pulse and almost no blood pressure.

AUSTRIA—A man was admitted to the ER after nailing his own testicle to a roof while doing repairs. The patient, who is fifty-nine, shot the four-inch nail into his left testicle with a compressed air gun and was unable to extract it or pull away from the roof. Emergency medics were called to separate the man and transport him to the hospital.

Surprise Party

The best one I remember was when I was in Buffalo. A woman gave birth to twins. She and her husband seemed so happy. He never let go of her hand until the second twin came out. The first was black and the second was white. It's very rare but it can happen. She had sex the same night with two men. All I can say is it was quite dramatic and after nurses took the distraught husband away, every doctor came by to look.

—Anonymous

Close the Door

An elderly woman was being transported to an alternate hospital in an ambulance. The paramedics were talking to her when the ambulance doors flew open while they were heading up a hill. The gurney she was strapped to flew out, rolled down the hill at tremendous speed, before tipping over, narrowly missing two cars traveling in the opposite direction.

—Anonymous

First Day on the Job

In 1982, my career, and the hospital I was working at, were just taking off. I was still on the day shift, but began working weekends as well. Through a training program, we had this temp that was a former gangbanger, but was trying to turn his life around. His name was Victor.

Sam, a friend of mine, and a practical joker, decided to pull a fast one on Victor and here's how it went:

Victor was so excited that he was working in a hospital. When his supervisor gave him a pager it was as if he had won the lottery.

Victor was doing his afternoon rounds and was proudly showing off his pager when Sam put out the page: "Victor! Call rehab! Stat at x2364."

The traction room is really 2364, but Victor didn't realize this and took the page and called in. Sam was waiting for the call and picked up the phone and said, "This is Barry down here in rehab, and we're in the middle of a procedure and Dr. James needs a fallopian tube STAT!"

The nurses started cracking up, anticipating what would happen next.

Since this is Victor's first important mission, he blasts down the halls into Central yelling, "I need a fallopian tube! Danny, I need a fallopian tube . . . right now!"

I laughed, gave him a brief lesson about the birds and the bees, and told him that Sam was pulling a fast one. I described what a fallopian tube was, but he was so pumped up he just didn't get it. So, I gave him the first tube I could find which was a Blakemore tube and told him to *run* with it.

Since you had to go through 3-F to get to rehab, Victor sped through the place as if it was a Code 3—Stat! The nurses were rolling hysterically.

Victor continued down the halls and into rehab where they were conducting business as usual and completely unaware of what was happening. He skidded into the room waving this Blakemore tube like a captured enemy flag in paintball, yelling, "Here's your fallopian tube! Here's your fallopian tube!"

—Danny, Northridge, California

Bizarre Physical Abnormalities

Athetosis—Constant involuntary movements of the hands and feet.

Contagious follicular keratosis—An extremely rare condition when the body becomes covered with small spinelike growths of a dirty yellow color. The spines are very hard.

Diphallic terata—The rare deformity of male genitals used to describe a man with two penises

Harlequin fetus—A newborn child is born covered with crusty fatty tissues. This is a severely disfiguring genetic disorder that involves thickened, ridged, and cracked skin that forms horny plates over the entire body, and distorts the facial features and constricts the digits. It is usually fatal in the first few days of life because the skin is so thick that the baby can't suck.

Nevus pilosus—These are enormous moles or birthmarks with great amounts of hair growing out of them. Oftentimes, the "bearded woman" or the "orangutan man" seen at carnivals, freak shows, or fairs are victims of this disorder.

Polyorchidism—This is the presence of more than two testicles, and is the opposite of the condition known as anorchidism, whereby a male is born with no testicles at all.

Saltatoric spasm—Chorea is an irregular, rapid, uncontrolled, involuntary, excessive movement that seems to move randomly from one part of the body to another. It causes the sufferer to spring up or jump about uncontrollably every time he or she attempts to stand.

Did They Really Say That?

MEDICAL RECORDS

The patient had waffles for breakfast and anorexia for lunch.

The patient was in his usual state of good health until his airplane ran out of gas and crashed.

Since she can't get pregnant with her husband, I thought you would like to work her up.

She is numb from her toes down.

While in the ER, she was examined, X-rated, and sent home.

The skin was moist and dry.

Occasional, constant, infrequent headaches.

Coming from Detroit, this man has no children.

Santa Claus from Hell

Sometimes you wonder why you became a doctor. One of the few times I thought about that was when I was an intern. There was this big, ornery guy—white beard, full head of white hair, and a big belly with raging diabetes. He had thick bloody sores on the bottom of his feet and he never bathed.

When sores are this bad we put live maggots on them and wrap them up. The maggots eat the dead skin and leave the healthy skin alone. Well, this guy got great joy out of unwrapping the bandage just as we finished and the maggots would fall to the floor and scurry around—we spent the next twenty minutes chasing maggots. We then put a cast on him and he left the hospital in his wheelchair. He went across the street, bought a bottle of Thunderbird, and then peed into his cast. He thought that was really funny. About an hour later he came back and asked us to change it. Nice night.

—**Dr. Zee, Chatsworth, California**

Misery—Sequel

A very thin fifty-five-year-old man came into the ER with broken ribs. As the story was told, he literally had to escape from his nearly three-hundred-pound wife who had inadvertently rolled onto him while sleeping—and fractured his ribs. She was ashamed of her weight problem and what she had done and refused to let her husband leave their apartment. A few days later, while she was sleeping, he broke out and hobbled straight to the hospital.

—Anonymous

Not Mine

A woman presented herself to the ER with stomach pains. When the doctor examined her he saw blood between her legs. He spread her legs a little and then he noticed a baby! "Oh my gosh, why didn't you tell me your were pregnant?" The woman replied, "That's not mine."

—Dr. George, Ann Arbor, Michigan

Up, Up, and Away!

A middle-aged couple was admitted to the emergency room: the wife for hysteria and her husband with a head injury. Apparently, a cousin, who had been unable to reach them, called the police who came and broke down their door.

When they entered the bedroom, they found the woman gagged, handcuffed, and tied to the bed. Her husband was unconscious on the floor wearing a Captain America outfit. The couple had been involved in a superhero role-playing fantasy game and the husband knocked himself out while attempting to jump onto his wife from the top of the television cabinet.

—Anonymous

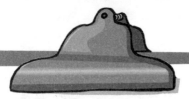

IT'S HOW YOU WANT TO LOOK AT IT

✓ The AMA, which is the acronym for the American Medical Association is also the acronym for Against Medical Advice.

✓ *WARNING:* If you hear a doctor call for a BE, get ready for a barium enema. If you hear PR, it's coming rectally.

✓ *WARNING* (part 2): If you hear a doctor state CTD, it's not a good thing. CTD is the acronym for Close to Death.

✓ *The Famous B's*
    BM = Bowel movement
    BS = Bowel sounds
    BT = Bowel tones
    BRP = Bathroom privileges

The Pregnant Man

One night in June 2006, Sanju Bhagat, a thirty-six-year-old farmer, was rushed to the hospital and admitted for severe abdominal pains and shortness of breath. Initially, doctors first thought that a giant tumor was pressing on his diaphragm and that accounted for his shortness of breath.

The man looked as if he was nine months pregnant and doctors were concerned about what kind of damage the tumor could be doing.

"I can usually spot a tumor just after I begin to operate, but this time I saw something I had never encountered," said Dr. Mehta. "As I cut deeper into Bhagat's stomach, gallons of fluid spilled out—and then something extraordinary happened. To my surprise and horror, I could shake hands with somebody inside. It was a bit shocking for me."

As reported, one limb came out, then another, some hair, more limbs, and a jaw.

There was a strange half-formed creature inside his stomach that had feet and hands, with long fingernails, and they were very developed.

At first, the doctors were stunned and it looked as if Bhagat had given birth, but actually, doctors had removed the mutated body of Bhagat's twin brother from his stomach.

DOCTORS

DR. JOHN HEINE *(urologist)*

———

DR. GARY RICKETTS

———

DR. JOHN SPINE

———

DR. CYNTHIA RASCH

———

DR. BONNIE BEAVER *(gynecologist)*

———

DR. LANA CAIN

———

DR. EDMOND LIPP

———

DR. PHILLIP HIPPS

———

DR. EVAN LIPKISS

———

The condition is rare and is actually called fetus in fetu, which is when a fetus is trapped inside its twin. The trapped fetus can survive as a parasite for sometime until it grows so large that it starts to harm the host. According to sources, there are fewer than ninety cases of fetus in fetu recorded.

—Various news sources

Rat Fink

In Florida, a man was admitted to the ER with lacerations on the tip of his penis. He was out of his mind and very upset. He claimed his wife had . . . "a rat in her privates" and it bit him during sex. Upon examining the woman, it was discovered that during a previous surgery, a surgical needle was left inside.

—Anonymous

City to Stay Clear of

Herpes—France

Bite the Bullet

In the OC, the real Orange County, California, a woman entered the ER complaining of a stomachache and a foul metal taste in her mouth. The patient had swallowed two 9mm bullets while eating a hot dog that she bought from a concession stand. She passed them naturally.

—Anonymous

NEWS AROUND THE WORLD

BERLIN, GERMANY—A hospital patient was trapped for three days in a hospital elevator after sneaking away from his bed for a cigarette.

Hospital staff and relatives searched for the patient, who was sixty years old and confined to a wheelchair.

The patient and his family plan to take legal action.

WICHITA, KANSAS—A twenty-three-year-old man walked into the ER after a botched kidnapping ended with him shooting himself in the left testicle.

The man had just stuck the gun back into his waistband when it fired, shooting himself. He cringed, causing the gun to fire again and strike him in the left calf.

Upon treatment, he and his two accomplices were arrested for aggravated attempted kidnapping and conspiracy to obstruct justice.

LILLINGTON, NORTH CAROLINA—A thirty-four-year-old man was admitted to the Betsy Johnson Regional Hospital in Dunn, North Carolina, after a woman tried to tear off his genitals with her hands at a Christmas party.

The patient needed fifty stitches and was released. His attacker was charged with malicious castration, assault causing serious bodily injury, malicious conduct, and injury to personal property.

GRAYS HARBOR, WASHINGTON—When seventy-seven-year-old Mae Bryson was told by doctors that she wasn't doing very well, there was one thing she wanted before she died. It was to see her grandson get married.

She was able to get her wish with a lot of help, but it took some complicated maneuvering to make it happen. The couple had to round up their six sons, get quick haircuts, find a minister, and all report to Room 6 in the ER where the wedding took place to the sounds of snoring patients and beeping monitors. In the end it proved to be a very happy day.

AUCKLAND, NEW ZEALAND—A

twenty-seven-year-old woman was admitted to Auckland Hospital's ER after she sustained serious injuries from being hit by a leaping dolphin near Slipper Island in the western reaches of the Bay of Plenty.

A spokesman for Auckland rescue said the woman was sitting in the bow of her small pleasure craft when the dolphin miscalculated its leap. The woman incurred a number of injuries and was admitted to the intensive care unit.

VALLEJO, CALIFORNIA—A fifty-nine-year-old man was admitted to the UC Davis Medical Center with second- and third-degree burns. Fire department officials said that a cell phone apparently had ignited in the man's pocket and started a fire that burned his hotel room and caused severe burns over half his body.

TULSA, OKLAHOMA—She thought she was fat and that losing weight was impossible. After years of diets that never worked, it was discovered that a thirty-two-year-old woman was carrying a ninety-three-pound tumor around with her.

"I quit going to doctors. Every one I went to told me to lose weight and I tried every diet I could think of," said Taquela Hilton.

Her primary care doctor Jennifer Cameron finally figured out that it wasn't just a problem with food, and an exploratory surgery was planned. It was during this surgery that doctors made the startling discovery. Since the surgery, Taquela has lost 137 pounds and her health is improving daily.

Hot Wax

A patient was brought to the ER after returning home from having a hot wax treatment at her local beauty shop. Her husband was alarmed when he saw that the skin around her eyes was darkened making her look like she had two black eyes. On top of that, the beautician removed layers of skin and flesh from her top lip after undergoing a hair-removal procedure. Ouch!

—Anonymous

Surprise, Surprise

A twenty-six-year-old woman was admitted into the hospital complaining of several days of abdominal pain. When told she was about to give birth, she said, "I didn't know, I didn't know." She had attributed the thirty-pound weight gain to rich food. Her boyfriend said, "I'm shocked." I guess so.

—Anonymous

Best Friends

A man had an altercation with a close friend who shot him in the head. The bullet went in and out and through his frontal lobe. He spent a few days in the ICU in the neurosurgery service. Once stable, he was transferred to a regular floor. The blast and the mechanism of the injury had given him essentially a frontal lobotomy, so his personality and mental status were clearly affected.

Despite having three separate "nurse sitters" in his room, who were watching over him, he managed to leave and find a pay phone. He called his "friend," the one who shot him, asking him to give him a ride home. His friend came to the hospital, picked him up, took him to his home, and shot him in the head again.

Unfortunately, he did not survive this time.

—Dr. Lara, Alameda, California

Payday Night

As a young intern, I accepted a "moonlight" job at a small Catholic community hospital in an industrial town. Once a week I would spend the night at the hospital on call for the emergency room.

One night, I was introduced to "payday night." The local steel mill, which hired fully 50 percent of the working population in the community, paid its employees every other Friday. The money in their pockets always led a few of the men into "living it up" from one bar to the next. On "payday night" fights would eventually ensue, and along about ten or eleven in the evening, the carnage would start to appear in the ER.

My first "payday night" was my worst. It had been a drunken and bloody fight, and the police kept bringing them in. I had my hands full, calling the doctors, sewing and patching. One man had been slashed badly in the neck, several vertical cuts running from chin to Adam's apple. Miraculously the jugulars were intact. The general practitioner on call was sure I could handle it. No anesthetic was required. The patient was stretched out on the emergency room table, and fell into a drunken sleep. I began the laborious task of putting the shredded skin back together again. I was about half finished when there was another flurry at the emergency room door. Several additional patients, bruised, battered, and bleeding from various points, were brought in by the police. They were also carrying a young man who was clutching his stomach.

"Uh oh," I thought, "Now the fat's in the fire. That one looks seriously injured."

I deserted my surgical patient, and ripping off my gloves went over to where the two officers had laid the young man on an examining table. He was curled into a ball, both arms tightly around his abdomen.

"What happened to him?" I asked.

"Took one in the stomach," said one of the officers.

"Took what? Did someone hit him?"

The officer smiled. "Yeah, with a bullet, Doc. He's gut shot of alcohol."

His pulse was steady, his color was a little pale, but he wasn't in shock. He only grunted when asked questions. I instructed the nurse to start plasma, the blood bank technician to draw blood for typing, cross-matching, and checking blood counts, and the clerk to telephone the physician on call. Meanwhile, I wanted to get a look at the wound so that I could describe where it was when I talked to the doctor.

But the young man refused to unfold his arms from across his abdomen. No argument would cause him to loosen his grip on his stomach. I finally asked the officers to help pry the arms loose. After they managed to get his arms down by his side, I was surprised not to see blood. But there was none. I loosened the man's belt, opened the zipper of his pants, and pulled up his shirt. Still, no blood. I pulled down his shorts. No injury or bleeding could be seen. After a thorough examination, not a scratch could be found.

The explanation was forthcoming later. It seemed that in the middle of a fight, the patient's opponent had pulled a gun, pushed it against the patient's abdomen, and pulled the trigger. There was a loud explosion and the patient had immediately fallen down, grasping his stomach. But when the police examined the gun later, they found it loaded with blanks.

It was impossible to convince the patient that he was not shot in the stomach. The last I saw of him he was being carried by two officers, still clasping his stomach, on his way to spend the night in jail to sleep it off.

—**Dr. George, Ann Arbor, Michigan**

Baby catcher—obstetrician

BoneHo—off-service resident working on orthopedic service

Captain Kangaroo—head of a pediatrics department

Cath jockey—This is a cardiologist who catheterizes every patient they see—or one who does cardiac catherizations.

Flea—internal medicine doctor

Freud squad—psychiatry department

Gasser, gas passer, *or* gas man—anesthesiologist

Dear Dr. Blatter,

Thank you for referring Mrs. Nabs to our office. Her leaking occurs with coughing, sneezing, and exercise, such as running. She would like to do more exercise, but the incontinence inhibits her. She does, however, continue to swim.

Very truly yours,
Dr. Dibick

Snap, Crackle, Pop

A twenty-nine-year-old man heard a snap during sexual intercourse, followed by immediate swelling and pain due to a penile fracture. This is not as uncommon as one would think. Guys do it when they are overly aggressive and miss the target.

—Anonymous

Yaba Daba Do

The patient dropped her husband off for his first day of work and was later admitted into the ER with a head wound. It seems in addition to a good-bye kiss, she flashed her breasts at him. She wasn't sure why she did it—just for fun—but she thought no one would see it. However, there was a cab driver that did see it and lost control of his cab, jumping the curb and running into the corner of the medical building. Inside, a dental technician was cleaning a patient's teeth. The crash made her jump and she tore the patient's gums with a cleaning pick. Shocked, he bit down, severing two of her fingers. All four people involved were admitted into the same ER.

—Retold from several sources

Medical Slang

In hospitals across the world, doctors, nurses, and technicians have created their own slang. Here are a few examples compiled from Web sites, news sources, magazines, and personal accounts that have been passed on from doctor to doctor. This is only a small sampling.

Acute lead poisoning—multiple gunshot wounds

ADR—ain't doin' it right

Angel lust—a male cadaver with an erection

Bash cash—insurance money used to pay for an accident

Bean—kidney

Blown mind—gunshot wound to the head

Bobbing for apples—a term used for using the finger to unclog a severely constipated patient

Bordeaux—urine with blood in it

Brain fry—electroconvulsive therapy, ECT. It is used for patients with severe depression.

Bugs in the rug—pubic lice

Bull in the ring—a blocked large intestine

Acronyms

AHF	acute hissy fit
ART	assuming room temperature (a patient died)
BMW	bitch, moan, and whine
CATS	cut all to shit
C/C	cancel Christmas (dead)
CTD	circling the drain (expected to die soon)
D&D	divorced and desperate—a middle-aged woman who regularly visits the hospital to seek male attention
DB	dirt ball (dirty person)
DBI	dirtbag index—a number calculated from number of tattoos and missing teeth

Can You Hear Me Yet? Part 2

The patient was released from a trauma center after having a cell phone removed from his rectum. "My dog drags the thing all over the house," he said later. "He must have dragged it into the shower. I slipped on the tile, tripped against the dog, and sat down right on the thing." The extraction took more than three hours due to the fact that the cover to the patient's phone had opened during insertion. Three times during the extraction his phone rang and each time, he made jokes about it that just had us rolling on the floor. By the time we finished, we really did expect to find an answering machine in there.

—From various sources

Spanish

A doctor who spoke limited Spanish rushed to a car in the ER parking lot to find a Spanish woman in the process of giving birth. He wanted to tell the woman to push, so he started yelling "*Puta! Puta! Puta!*" Then the grandmother started to cry and the baby's father had to be restrained. What the doctor should have been saying was "*Puja!*" (Push!) Instead he said, "Whore! Whore! Whore!"

—**Anonymous**

I Knew That

A young female patient came to the ER with lower abdominal pain. She was given a pregnancy test anyway and it came back positive. The patient was given the results and asked again if she was sexually active.

To our surprise she said, "Sexually active? No, sir, I just lay there." She was asked if she knew who the father was and she said, "No. Who?"

—Anonymous

Cover Your Mouth
When You Cough

A young patient presented herself with a persistent cough, sputum, and fever for the preceding six months. Despite a trial of antibiotics and antituberculosis treatments, her symptoms did not improve. A subsequent X-ray showed a nonhomogeneous collapse-consolidation of the right upper lobe. A detailed retrospective history confirmed an accidental inhalation of a condom.

—Anonymous

NEWS AROUND THE WORLD

ROSEVILLE, CALIFORNIA—A Roseville woman was admitted to the ER after being pinned to the floor for four days after her refrigerator fell on top of her in her kitchen. The sixty-nine-year-old woman's refrigerator was top heavy and as she leaned in to open the fridge door, it fell forward, toppling onto her.

The woman tried calling for help any way she could. At first, she grabbed some shattered glass pieces that fell on top of her during the accident and threw them at her kitchen window to draw attention and make noise. When that didn't work, she managed to grab a wooden spoon and a pressure-cooker lid, and banged the two together as she called for help.

On the fourth day, Greg Allen, a politician running for the Placer County Water Board, heard her call for help while going door-to-door campaigning. He found an unlocked door and ran in to save her life.

The patient suffered a broken collarbone, and injured both legs as a result of the accident. She says that she doesn't care which political party Allen represents, she's voting for him either way.

SHERIDAN, COLORADO—A couple was admitted to the Swedish Medical Center for burns, possible shrapnel wounds, and broken eardrums. For some reason the couple had filled a balloon with acetylene—a very explosive gas used for welding—so they could blow the balloon up for a Super Bowl party. On the drive, the balloon rolled across the backseat of the car, possibly causing static electricity that ignited it. Kabam!

PITTSBURGH, PENNSYLVANIA—Officials were perplexed when it was discovered that over $104,000 dollars worth of colonoscopes were stolen from Armstrong County Memorial Hospital in East Franklin Township. The scopes are used to examine the human colon.

MADRID, SPAIN—Spanish matador Fernando Cruz's future fatherhood is in question after suffering from two 25 centimeter long horn wounds. The handsome bullfighter was thrown in the air and when he hit the ground, a second bull gored him in the groin, eviscerating both testicles. Doctors operated for two hours and the young matador is scheduled to return to the ring in three weeks.

GAINSVILLE, FLORIDA—Taking a page out of Mike Tyson's book, a thirty-seven-year-old man was admitted to the ER after having his right ear bitten off by an angry neighbor. When paramedics arrived, they retrieved the separated ear but doctors were unable to reattach it.

UKRAINE—A Ukrainian man bit a grocer's ear off in a Siberian store when the clerk refused to give the guy a free watermelon. The earless man picked up his ear and was last seen heading toward the ER.

BAJA CALIFORNIA—A thirty-three-year-old woman was sail fishing with her friend when a blue marlin jumped out of the water and speared her right arm and chest. The woman was rushed to a local ER where doctors told her that her life had been saved by her silicone breast implants.

Just a Shine Please

A seventeen-year-old man was admitted with lacerations, discoloring, and bruises to his penis. His parents were embarrassed and angry with their son. They were well off and were staying in a suite at one of Houston's finest hotels, complete with its own electric shoe-shine machine. The young man had inserted his penis into the machine and it unexpectedly pulled it between the brushes and the mechanism—and . . . it got stuck.

—Anonymous

Misunderstanding

I am an operating room nurse in a midwestern hospital that shall remain nameless. We have, on our staff, an anesthesiologist who came to the USA from an Asian country. His command of English is fairly good, but he has trouble with American slang.

One day, as I was helping him place a spinal anesthetic in a patient who was to have prostate surgery, this problem, shall we say, came to a head.

I was supporting the patient, who was sitting up, but slouched over with his head tucked down, which is the optimum position for placing the needle through which the anesthetic is given. Before the spinal needle is introduced, the anesthesiologist usually numbs the skin and deeper tissues with a local medication such as you might get in a dentist's office.

Though given through a small needle, this medication can sting as it goes in, so we usually warn the patient that he is about to experience some discomfort.

As the anesthesiologist prepared to administer the local medication, he said, by way of warning, "Little prick here!"

At this, the patient shrugged his shoulders and said, "Yeah, I know. It's been that way all my life."

After the case, I took the anesthesiologist aside and suggested that in the future he use the phrase "bee sting" as a warning to his patients.

—Anonymous

Oh . . . My . . . God!

OK, so I wouldn't have believed this either, but I was working in the ER the day *this* guy came in.

He was about twenty, and he was *freaking* out when he arrived. The young man was crying, shaky, and reported that he had a weird thing growing in his throat and that it was making it difficult to breathe. His twin brother, who was with him also had similar complaints—and both were hyperventilating. The one twin reportedly looked in his mouth and saw the growth just prior to rushing them both into the ER. Before he left the house he asked his brother to look at it—and then his brother looked in his OWN mouth as well and saw that he had the same growth! It was then that the difficulties with breathing started, and they hightailed it to get emergency care. They figured out that they had both developed these growths in the same place because they were identical twins.

The nurse that triaged them could hardly contain herself. When she had calmed them down long enough to be able to look in the throat of the first twin, he cried out.

"Can you see it?!!! Can you see that red thing hanging down in the back of my mouth?"

Of course she could. These twins were distressed over discovering their uvulas, which we all have.

I guess some people don't have any awareness of their bodies.

—Anonymous

Be Careful of What You Say

A handsome thirty-five-year-old man came in for a colonoscopy. I tend to use Versed, an amnestic that allows the patient to be conscious but sedated during the procedure. Frequently this drug has a disinhibiting affect and the patient often says things during the procedure, which he or she would usually not otherwise say. In addition, the patient will not remember either the procedure or what they might have said.

In this case as we began to do the procedure the patient started talking about how his wife had not had sex with him in three years. He went on in detail about how frustrated he was and what she wouldn't do.

I had three young single nursing assistants with me, and they were horrified at how this handsome man's wife would not have sex with him.

A few weeks after the procedure the man came to my office for a follow-up. He said he couldn't remember a thing but he remarked how extremely friendly my nursing staff was.

—Dr. C.B., Encino, California

The Thumb

This story is funny, at least to me—in quite a strange way. It happened many years ago when I spent time on the surgical pathology bench. Frozen sections for immediate reading by the pathologist were common in those days—even though the tissue was much harder to interpret. I always hated them for their inaccuracy, as well as for not allowing circumspect judgment to be exercised by the operating surgeon.

This story involves a frozen section on a neurosurgeon's thumb, where the curettings from an erosive subungual (underneath the nail) lesion were mistakenly diagnosed as "squamous cell carcinoma," which is cancer. An amputation of the thumb was done minutes later. The usual practice was for all the senior people to confer on frozen sections, but the best surgical pathologist in the department was at lunch at the time, and when he returned shortly afterward and looked at the slide, he quickly said, "keratoacanthoma," and walked away. KAs tend to come and go in about a six-week stretch, so this lesion would likely have resolved spontaneously and certainly would not have progressed beyond its current extent. The story, to me, is instructive about rapid diagnosis, uncircumspect treatment, and medical error, even in how it does not spare medical insiders. This was the chairman of the neurosurgery department, and his operating career ended just like that!

—Anonymous

Good Old Hank

The patient interaction from my brief clinical days that I find funny, though a bit cruel, is this one, from my fourth year of medical school.

Our medical rotations were ten weeks, and my time on medicine was the second of four blocks. I inherited a patient from another student. I'll never forget his name, Hank, and that he was in his late eighties. I was very excited about him because he had been critically ill with hepatitis and no one thought he would live. But Hank had rallied and was doing well: coherent, sitting up in bed, animated, no longer jaundiced. He was a cheerful and talkative guy. He also was terribly hard of hearing and had a powerful hearing aid.

One morning on rounds—a serious affair, as I'm sure you know, with little time to shoot the breeze—our group of six students, an intern, a resident, and an attending doctor stopped by his bed to check in on him. We were tickled to see him happy, sitting with strength, in blooming rosy color. As I approached to ask him how he was doing Hank lifted his hand, palm out, as a gesture to indicate that I should wait until he put his hearing aid on. He fidgeted all over the place for at least five minutes as everyone patiently waited. Finally, he got it on by himself and turned it on. He looked at us in happy anticipation. I began the interaction but only mouthed the words. Poor Hank just sank, but when everyone laughed, he perked up immediately and his eyes twinkled as never before. Hank was discharged the next week, in great shape.

—Dr. Peters, Philadelphia, Pennsylvania

Acronyms

DFO	done fell out, used to describe fainting
FFDID	found facedown in ditch
FFDIG	found facedown in gutter
FLK	funny-looking kid
FLK with GLM	funny-looking kid with a good-looking mom
FOOBA	found on ortho barely alive
FOS	full of shit, describing severe constipation that can be seen on an X-ray of the abdomen
FUBAR	F**KED up beyond all repair; a patient who is so trauma-injured that he/she is beyond help. For example, the guy who tried to commit suicide by jumping thirty feet and landed on his head and was still breathing when he arrived at the ER.

Medical Slang

Bury the hatchet—when surgical instruments are accidentally left inside a
   patient

Celestial discharge—a nursing slang term for death

Chandelier sign—used to describe a patient who experiences extreme pain
   during a physical exam

Chocolate hostage—constipated

Code brown—when a patient poops in his or her bed

Code yellow—urination emergency

Crispy critter—a patient with severe burns

Crock—hypochondriac

Crook-U—the area in the hospital where they take the prisoners

Crump—to have a sudden change for the worse

Crump, gork, vedgy—a patient requiring intensive care, incapable of movement

Cut and paste—to open a patient, discover that there is no hope, and immediately
   sew him up. It has been reported that in some cases, young surgeons
   practice surgical techniques for a while before closing the patient.

Dance—This is the process of tying a surgical gown behind the surgeon's back,
   involving a 180-degree spin by the surgeon. "Shall we dance?"

Dandruff on wheels—a patient with a flaky or infectious skin condition

Pest Control

A long time ago I had a patient, a nice woman in her late sixties who had a recurring bout of phlebitis, which is generally an inflammation of a vein in the leg. When I told her the diagnosis, she looked up at me and said, "That's no problem, I got some Raid when the 'FLEA-BITE-US.'"

—Anonymous

Interesting Choice of Words
- Davies Diabetes, Professional Ass
- In a hospital's maternity ward: No Children Allowed.

Just Yucky

One of our attending doctors approached a nursing student with a guiac card (a card that contains a fecal swab to determine if the patient has blood present) and asked her if she thought there was blood. The young nurse said she wasn't sure. The doctor agreed with her and then turned the card over and tasted the stool sample and stated, "no blood here." The nursing student let out a little yell and walked quickly out of the department. The stool sample was actually bean dip.

—Dr. Mandrachi, Oakland, California

Read the Sign, Dude

One afternoon we heard the sound of someone running fast through the ER. When we looked up, we saw the doctor step back calmly and watch as a young man with hair standing straight up raced down the hall with three police officers on his heels. He had escaped from the jail ward. The next sound we heard was BAM! It was the sound of the young man slamming into the door to the exit of the ER at full force. The police simply picked him up and took him back to his bed. The door he hit was the security door and the metal handle had to be pushed on to open the door. He had no idea. But he did now.

—Margo, RN, Alameda, California

A Name Is Just a Name

To keep things light, we name the areas of the ER with special names. We keep all the psych patients in what is called the "gulag." We send the cardiac patients to the "barn" where they are hooked up to monitors and of course, my favorite, the "pelvatoriaum," do I need to say more?

—Dr. Tee, Alameda, California

FACT

✓ An estimated 107 million Americans needed to visit an emergency room in the past year.

✓ In a landmark government study, nearly a million people wind up in the emergency room after using medicines.

Medical Slang

The deep fry—cobalt therapy

Departure lounge—geriatric ward

Digging for worms—varicose vein removal surgery

The dotted "Q"—the "Q" sign, with a fly on the tongue

Drooler—a catatonic patient

Dump—to arrange for a patient who should probably be admitted to your service to be dumped onto another service

Eating in—intravenous feeding

Fascinoma—a "fascinating" tumor, any interesting or amusing malignancy

Four F-er—a gallbladder patient. "Fat, fortyish, flatulent, female"

God's waiting room—geriatric ward

Gomer—a senile, messy, or highly unpleasant patient (Or an acronym of "Get out of my emergency room!")

Gone camping—a patient in an oxygen tent

Gorillacillin—a powerful antibiotic

Gorked—The patient is unresponsive and nonverbal. "The patient is gorked out."

Hallucinoma—This is a term used when you thought you saw something that wasn't really there.

Picasso

A psych patient ran out of the ER and barged into our nurse manager's office. He then pulled out his IV and lovingly decorated her walls with his blood. Some of the pictures were not bad.

—Tonya, RN, Oakland, California

The Baby

Although our standard diagnostic nomenclature in psychiatry covers many conditions, I never experienced this before. One night, a fifty-three-year-old male presented himself in the ER dressed as a baby. He carried a bottle and had on a soiled diaper. There were no aggressive undertones with this behavior. He talked in a childlike voice yet had some concept that he was indeed not a baby.

Apparently, while at work he was completely normal, but being a baby so much of the time outside of work was beginning to cause him significant anxiety and have an effect on his personal relationships. This man was insistent that he be taken from the ER to the nursery where he could be with the other babies. I told him I couldn't do that because he was in fact not a baby. At this time, he fell to the floor and had a complete tantrum.

—Anonymous

Burn Baby Burn

A Croatian woman, who lived in Zada, suffered burns to her buttocks after lightning struck her in her mouth and passed through her body. The young woman was in her home brushing her teeth when the lightning struck.

"I had just put my mouth under the tap to rinse away the toothpaste when lightning must have struck the building. I don't remember anything after that but I was later told that the lightning had traveled down the water pipe and struck me on the mouth passing through my body."

Doctors admitted her to the ER and said, "The accident is bizarre but not impossible."

She was wearing rubber bathroom shoes at the time so instead of exiting out her feet it took a turn and exited out her backside. The shoes clearly saved her life. If she hadn't been wearing the shoes, she might have died. She made a full recovery.

—Retold from European news sources

A Shot in the Ass

A trauma patient, brought in on a night shift, said he had been shot in the butt a half hour prior to calling the paramedics. The team asked him why he waited before calling them. The patient stated that he heard the gunshots but did not feel pain or see blood—so he went home and took a bath. When he was in the tub he saw blood and then called 911. After a further exam, it was learned that the patient had never been shot—he had a humongous hemorrhoid that was bleeding. GROSS.

—Dr. T., San Francisco, California

Nightmare

One of the trauma chiefs was catching a nap on a chair in the corner. All of a sudden, he started twitching and yelling, "NO! NO! PLEASE DON'T." We started laughing because he was clearly having a bad dream. One of the nurses went over to wake him. He jumped out of the chair and assumed a karate position. His eyes were wide open—attentive, ready for action. When he realized it was just a dream, he said he had dreamed that he was being held down by the nurses and they were putting a tube in every place they could.

—Dr. M., Los Angeles, California

Hello?

A forty-six-year-old man came into the ER with a burned ear and cheek. The story went this way. He said, "My wife was ironing while I was watching the Stanley Cup. There were a few minutes left in the game. She had left the iron next to the phone and when it rang, I picked up the iron instead of the phone."

—Anonymous

Medical Slang

Hammered—This is when a doctor gets a bunch of admits while on call. "I got hammered last night with ten admissions."

Head bonk—describes an otherwise uninjured patient who was struck on the head but came to the ER just to be sure

Healthy goober—a dead patient

Hey Docs—Alcoholics handcuffed to wheelchairs calling out, "Hey, Doc!" at the sight of any white coat

Hit and run—operating quickly so the doctor can get to his golf game or other appointment

Hole-in-one—a gunshot wound through the mouth or rectum

"I fell on it."—This is an answer patients give for how a foreign object got into their rectum.

IHOP *or* International House of Pancakes—usually the stroke ward full of patients all babbling in a different incoherent language

Knife and gun club—This is a term used in county hospitals in the inner city where their trauma units see a lot of gunshot and knife wounds.

Last flea to jump off a dead dog—This is a term used to describe an oncologist who never seems to be able to let people die with dignity.

Loop the loop—a complicated surgical rearrangement of the intestines

Loose change—a dangling limb in need of amputation

NEWS AROUND THE WORLD

ROMANIA—A thirty-eight-year-old woman was admitted to the ER with abdominal pains after swallowing her lover's false teeth in a moment of passion. The woman was reluctant to tell doctors what had happened and they were surprised when the X-ray showed false teeth in her stomach.

After spending two days in the hospital, the foreign object exited her body the natural way.

OHIO—A pilot and his passenger were treated at a local ER for minor injuries after their single-engine aircraft crashed on takeoff. During a postcrash investigation a wasp nest was found under the pilot's seat. Since the pilot was allergic to bee stings, he passed out after being stung several times during takeoff and crashed.

SOUTH CAROLINA—A pilot in a Hughes HU-269 helicopter was flying an aerial observation flight when he turned on the cockpit heat and was shocked to see a copperhead snake emerge from the vent near his feet. As the pilot maneuvered toward a landing area, the snake appeared, poised to strike. The pilot tried to step on the snake with his foot and subsequently lost control of the helicopter. The helicopter hit some trees before crashing to the ground. The pilot was injured and rushed to a local hospital.

Brain Food

A seventy-year-old man was admitted to a northern California ER after being in an automobile accident. The man was suffering from an unusual form of cancer that had eaten away the upper portion of his skull. Apparently he had not sought any medical treatment because the condition was not causing him pain. He sort of just let it fester. When the paramedic found him, he was surprised to see a large portion of his skull had been eaten away by maggots and they were now eating and crawling around his brain.

—Anonymous

Size Doesn't Matter

When I was a resident in Alabama, a distinguished older man entered the ER complaining about his inability to urinate. After an examination, I told him he needed to undress so I could catherize him. The man unzipped his pants and my eyes looked down and I saw the largest penis I had ever seen. I was so impressed by the length and girth of his penis I forgot to ask him how long he had had the urinary problem and instead asked him how long his penis was.

—Anonymous

Beware of Dog

A patient in his early thirties was treated in the ER for dog bites to the upper thigh and the skin of his left testicle. We knew there was something fishy when we examined him and his injuries didn't match up because his pants showed no evidence of a tear.

The story just didn't add up. While getting a history of the patient, he finally confessed what had really happened.

He was having sex with a married woman while her husband was out of town. Suddenly, out of the blue, the absent landlord's dog showed up in the room and jumped at him from behind, catching his thigh in the process. His story finally fit the injury.

Unfortunately, a police report has to be filed for every dog bite in the county. As soon as he found out about this, the obviously embarrassed guy promptly left the ER before the police showed up.

—Retold from various sources

Stick in the Mud

It was midnight when we heard that a jumper went off the Cry Baby Bridge and was on his way to the ER. He was a twenty-six-year-old male who had been distressed due to personal problems.

He stood on top of the bridge, which he later said looked like he was on top of the Empire State Building, and took what he thought was his final leap. He landed feet first in a ten-foot swamp full of bayou sludge. He was stuck there for about ten hours until a passing car heard him cry for help. The guy broke his ankle and left foot.

—Anonymous

Acronyms

GLF	ground-level fall, when someone trips or falls from a standing or sitting position
GOK	God only knows; confession medical staff makes when no one knows what the patient's illness is
GPO	good for parts only as in, "Save the good parts only."
GSW	gunshot wound
LGFD	looks good from door; used to describe a difficult patient who you do not want to enter the room and interact with
LOBNH	lights on but nobody home—stupid
LOL	little old lady

Medical Slang

Marriageable monster—a young female patient who has successfully undergone major plastic surgery

Meth mouth—a finding among patients severely addicted to methamphetamine

OBS and GOBS—obstetrics and gynecology

Oligoneuronal—stupid (means "small number of brain cells")

The "O" sign—The letter "O" as formed by a patient's gaping mouth. This is oftentimes seen with very sick or old patients.

Peek and shriek—to open a patient surgically, discover an incurable condition, and close the incision immediately

Pinky cheater—latex finger cover used in gynecological and proctological examinations

Pneumo-cephalic—an airhead or stupid person

Pop drop—dropping off a parent at a care facility

Pumpkin positive—lacking in intelligence. This implies that the patient's brain is so small that shining a torch into their mouth would cause their head to light up like a pumpkin.

The "Q" sign—a patient giving the "O" sign with his tongue hanging out

Road map—when an accident victim goes through the windshield of a car face first

Be Careful What You Ask For

A group of older women got together once a month for a special activity. Sometimes it was to go to a movie, sometimes to a museum. On this Saturday, a seventy-seven-year-old woman was rushed into the ER in full cardiac arrest and soon expired on the table. Apparently, the group had visited a tarot card reader and shortly after the reader told this woman that she could see no future in her cards, the woman collapsed with a heart attack and died.

—Dr. Marlo, Rancho Mirage, California

Great Restaurant

Heart Attack Grill—Home of the Double Bypass Burger is located in Tempe, Arizona, and serves a yummy burger with tons of fat and cholesterol. Not for the faint of heart.

The Human Couch

A woman with shortness of breath and weighing nearly five hundred pounds was brought into the ER on a tarp and carried by six firemen. While being undressed, an asthma inhaler fell out of one of the folds under her arm. After an X-ray showed a round mass on the left side of her chest her massive left breast was lifted to find a shiny new dime. And last but not least, during a pelvic exam, a TV remote control was discovered in one of the folds of her crotch. She became known as "The Human Couch."

—From various sources

Bing Bang

A thirty-five-year-old male was transported to our ER by rescue unit from his doctor's office.

The patient had complained to his physician of decreased appetite, restlessness, and confusion for the last three days. The man stated that he had been working under the hood of his car and had leaned on the battery, causing an arc which sent him crashing to the ground and striking the back of his head.

The man returned home that day and told his wife about the accident. His wife noted an "abrasion" to the back of his skull, and cleaned the wound. However, over the next three days, he became increasingly confused, anorexic, and at times agitated.

The man's physician deemed it necessary to obtain a CT scan and further evaluation, and ordered transport to the ER. On arrival to the department, the ER physician ordered the CT of the brain, concluding that perhaps the patient had suffered a brain injury, which was secondary to the original accident. As the patient's primary nurse, I went to fetch the patient from CT.

I asked the CT technician, who was noticeably worried, for a preliminary reading. "There is a bullet in his brain." Incredulous, I returned the patient to the ER with the news, and the definitive reading came minutes later—foreign body located between the hemispheres, likely a bullet.

Apparently, the man had not been arced by the battery, but had been shot in the back of the head with a handgun, and was not aware of this fact! The patient was admitted to ICU, but no surgery was performed—the neurosurgeon felt that the procedure was too risky.

He survived and was discharged ten days later.

—**Anonymous**

The South African
Floor Polisher Massacre

Every Friday over a period of months, hospital staff found that a patient who occupied a certain bed in intensive care was dead— with no apparent cause. At first it seemed like a coincidence, but when the deaths continued the doctors feared a "killer disease."

Finally, a nurse noticed the Friday cleaning lady doing her weekly chores. This maid would enter the ward, unplug the life-support system beside the bed, plug in her floor polisher, clean the ward, and once again plug in the patient, leaving no trace of the cause of the patient's death.

How many died in the South African Floor Polisher Massacre? The Free State Health and Welfare Department won't comment but is investigating.

—Retold from various sources

My Scalpel Is
Bigger Than Yours!

At a Massachusetts medical center, two surgeons fell out during a laparoscopy.

Nurses started screaming in fright, but this didn't put off the two pugilists. As tensions grew, the doctors actually tried to stab each other with their scalpels.

Eventually they calmed down and finished the operation. The patient survived and the Massachusetts authorities ordered both surgeons to undergo psychotherapy.

—Anonymous

Love Those Lungs

Here's one that really did happen in our hospital. A very pretty Swedish medical student was admitted to the medical ward suffering from pneumonia. During the professorial ward round the Houseman was asked to inspect the lady's chest for abnormal breath sounds. Having just come out of his final exam and remembering that one had to examine the chest free from clothes, he sheepishly asked the patient/medical student to undress. He then examined her with his stethoscope, and all was going well until he noted that everybody was in hysterics. The female student asked him if he might wish to listen to her lungs again, but this time with the stethoscope in his ears.

—Anonymous

Those Boots Were Made for Walkin'

We were called for a man who had just bought a pair of cowboy boots to wear to the Friday night poker game. Since the boots were new, they were hard to get on and off. The man developed an itch on his ankle and—being a bright man with three beers in him—went out to the kitchen and got a long and very sharp knife. He slid the knife repeatedly into the boot, and soon the itching disappeared. Later, when someone went to get another beer, a large puddle of blood was found under the table. By the time we got there, the patient was clearly in shock. The patient lived, but to bandage his leg, we had to cut the boot off.

—Anonymous

Did They Really Say That?

MEDICAL RECORDS

Patient was alert and unresponsive.

When she fainted, her eyes rolled around the room.

This patient has been under many psychiatrists in the past.

The pelvic examination will be done later on the floor.

She was divorced last April. No other serious illness.

Dr. Johnson is watching his prostate.

The patient was advised not to go around exposing himself to other people.

STRANGE NAMES FOR
DOCTORS

Dr. Charles Paine

Dr. Maroon Dick

Dr. Michael Achey

Dr. H'doubler Peter

Dr. David Dickoff

Dr. Dan Medic

Dr. James Busyhead

Dr. Charles Butts *(antismoking advocate)*

Dr. Offa Peanis *(circumcision expert)*

The Cue Tip

A husband and wife came into the ER screaming and yelling at each other. He had received a laceration to his face while chasing his wife around their home during an argument. She was furious and told us she was sick and tired of his continual accusations of her infidelity. She turned to her husband and said, "Tell them! Tell them what you think!"

The man then claimed that an illicit cue tip had impregnated his wife.

—Anonymous

Chainsaw Guy

I'm working in the ER one day when they bring in this guy on a stretcher. His pants are covered in blood and he's got this giant mess of muscle sticking out of a giant wound on his right thigh. He's also got a bandage on his left index finger. I ask him what happened. He said that he was using a chainsaw to cut some lumber when his coworker called his name. He turned, and, not paying attention to where the chainsaw was, nicked his left finger with it. The pain completely shocked him, and he dropped the chainsaw . . . onto his leg!

—Connie, RN, Detroit, Michigan

Happy Halloween

I was working the night shift in the ER in Greenwich Village on the night of the Halloween Parade. In this particular ER, the paramedics wheel patients into a receiving area where a registrar assigns them to beds. I was working on a patient when I heard the registrar behind me ask, "What do you got?"

The paramedic replied, "It looks like . . . a goblin and a zombie." I turned around and saw that they had two guys on stretchers: one in a goblin outfit and one in zombie makeup. The whole nursing station broke out in laughter. The night went on like this as various drunk people in costume were brought in.

—**Connie, RN, Detroit, Michigan**

Nice Friends

A guy walks into the ER in a trench coat and a spy hat. He said he was having a lot of pain. We asked him to disrobe and he refused. We told him we couldn't evaluate his pain without him taking his clothes off. He said he couldn't because he didn't want to lose his friends. He was not specific in telling us who his friends were. Finally, we were able to get him to agree to undress, and when he did his "friends" were revealed. He had hundreds of silverfish bugs crawling on his body . . . nice friends.

—Dr. Samuel, New York City, New York

A Bouncing Baby ****?

A sixty-year-old woman presented herself in the ER stating that she was pregnant. We knew this woman because she was a schizophrenic who had been in and out of the hospital several times. She was insistent that she was about to give birth to a baby. We knew she wasn't pregnant but gave her a pregnancy test that of course came back negative. We took her to X-ray and on the film it showed that she was horribly constipated. We gave her an enema and a bowel regimen and shortly thereafter she had a massive bowel movement. She said she was extremely happy that she was able to deliver "her baby."

—Dr. Samuel, New York City, New York

Staples

It was close to the end of the day. We were exhausted having had to complete a number of surgeries. There was this surgical resident that no one really liked, and he was already irritable and tired and now just wanted to go home. We got a call that they had added one more patient to the schedule. This was a "charity case"—no insurance—and it really pissed him off. The man was very obese and this is where the story starts.

The resident began to dress the patient for surgery, but each time he put the drape up on the stomach, it would slip off. The resident did this a few times, and each time it again slipped off. We could see he was getting more frustrated by the moment. Each time he set it and turned to do something else, it kept slipping off. The exasperated resident finally turned and picked up the staple gun and stapled the drape to the patient's stomach.

—Anonymous

Medical Slang

Roasted goober—a tumor after intensive cobalt treatment

Scratch and sniff—a gynecological examination

Sidewalk souffle—a patient who has fallen or jumped from a building and splattered on the ground

Silver goose, silver stallion—proctoscope

Slow code—This is when an older patient is very ill, but wants everything done so they will not die. Hospital personnel respond very slowly.

Slow code to China—same as above. "Don't hurry, the patient is a "slow 'boat' to China.""

Smashola—a patient with multiple blunt trauma injuries, usually a motor vehicle accident

Squash—brain

Tattoo titer—a way to measure the likelihood of a patient being insane. The assumption is the more tattoos on the patient, the more insane the patient is likely to be.

Tooth to tattoo ratio—a way to gauge the social and economic class of a patient presumed to be a hillbilly

Did They Really Say That?

MEDICAL RECORDS

The patient was somewhat agitated and had to be encouraged to feed and eat himself.

The patient developed a puffy right eye, which was felt to be caused by an insect bite by an ophthalmologist.

Apparently the mother resented the fact that she was born in her forties.

Physician has been following the patient's breast for six years.

He had a left-toe amputation one month ago. He also had a left-above-the-knee amputation last year.

If the Disease Won't Kill Ya . . .
the Hospital Will

A woman in her mid-twenties was admitted to the medical service for pancytopenia (very low white/red blood cells and platelets) and clinically palpable cervical lymphadenopathy (enlarged neck lymph nodes).

The surgical service was asked to perform a biopsy of the lymph nodes, as lymphoma was suspected and they needed tissue diagnosis to tailor chemotherapy, if indeed she had cancer.

The patient underwent the procedure under local anesthesia with IV sedation in the OR. She had a simple face mask delivering oxygen. The dissection was on the right posterior neck, when suddenly a low flame, likely caused by a spark while being cauterized, ignited with the oxygen. It was first seen on her chest, but quickly progressed toward the head. In a matter of seconds, a more pronounced flame, much like a torch, filled the face mask, and headed toward the patient's airway. Basically, the woman had flames shooting into her mouth and nose and down her throat.

The operation was terminated, the drapes quickly ripped away, the oxygen stopped, and the patient was incubated as she sustained second- and third-degree burns to her face and oropharynx (which includes the base of the tongue). The patient remained relatively stable and was then transferred to a burn center.

A few days later in the burn center, the admitting team requested a hematology consult since they still did not have a diagnosis for her pancytopenia. The hematologist decided to perform a bone marrow biopsy at the bedside, in the ICU, from the patient's sternum.

During the procedure, her right internal mammary artery was lacerated. The patient became hemodynamically unstable, and a right chest tube was inserted, revealing a large hemothorax (a rupture that caused blood to pour into the chest). A resuscitative thoracotomy (a surgical incision to the chest) was performed at the bedside; however, the patient already exsanguinated (or bled out) from the injury to the internal mammary artery and unfortunately expired. Both complications (the burn and the arterial injury) happened in the course of two purely elective operations. The patient died without ever establishing a diagnosis.

—Anonymous

Ice Cold

This is a once-in-a-lifetime case. In all my years in medicine, I've never seen another like it. A six-foot-four, three-hundred-pound man was brought into the ER. He was irritable and nasty. He was also extremely drunk with a blood alcohol level of .40, which is very dangerous and can be toxic. His core blood temperature was 87 degrees. This is unheard of. Most people would be dead at 91 degrees.

We didn't believe it when we took it orally and so we took it rectally and received the same result. Because of his size and the amount of alcohol he had consumed, his heart kept pumping and he survived. We warmed him up by microwaving saline solution.

—**Dr. Samuel, New York City, New York**

Knock, Knock

There was an old lady who was having a knee replacement. We gave her a drug called Ketamine, which is a dissociatative anesthetic. It's a drug that will keep the patient awake during the operation but disassociated from the procedure.

With this surgery, you need a mallet to bang the replacement into place. The surgeon started banging. BANG! BANG! BANG! The woman said, "Who's there?" We laughed and then the surgeon started banging again. BANG! BANG! BANG! She yelled out, "Will someone PLEASE get the door?"

—Dr. Samuel, New York City, New York

Do You Think I'm Nuts?

A psych patient and I argued about whether or not he was able to leave the hospital. He kept telling me if I kept him locked up he would kill himself. I told him as long as he kept threatening to kill himself, we had to keep him in the hospital where he would be safe. He argued that I should let him out so he could then kill himself outside of the hospital. He just never got it.

—Dr. Samuel, New York City, New York

Fire in the Hole—Part One

A young man rushed into the ER after a horrific firecracker accident that left him incontinent and unable to have sex.

The twenty-six-year-old man suffered a fractured pelvis and severe burns to his genital area after a firecracker exploded between the cheeks of his buttocks.

An ambulance was called to Dapto's Reed Park about 2:30 A.M. on August 10 after reports came in that a man was hemorrhaging from the buttocks. He was in serious but stable condition when he was admitted to the ER.

The injuries sustained from the accident were quite extensive and he required emergency surgery. Unfortunately the patient had a colostomy and a catheter, and was sexually dysfunctional.

Illawarra Health emergency surgeon Dr. Robert McCurdie, who operated on the patient, likened his condition to "a war injury."

—From various news sources

Fire in the Hole—Part Two

A twenty-two-year-old former soldier suffered internal injuries after lighting a small firecracker he had inserted into his buttocks and was immediately admitted into the ER.

The incident took place Sunday, when Britain celebrated Bonfire Night. This date is traditionally marked with fireworks to celebrate the Guy Fawkes' gunpowder plot to blow up Parliament in the seventeenth century.

—From various news sources, London, England

Calling Dr. Sweet

Most hospitals have secret codes attributed to certain situations. At our hospital, when we hear "paging Dr. Sweet," we know it's a security situation and generally I stay as far away as possible.

This night I had a patient in the ICU, brain dead and on a ventilator. She had a (DNR) "do not resuscitate," which meant that she didn't want any measures done to keep her alive. It was decided that it was time to take her off the ventilator and let her pass. Well, the family was a hillbilly type—a lot of tension between them. When it came time for them to say goodbye, the drunk 225-pound daughter with the missing front tooth stumbled in and picked a fight with her older brother. When the shouting started we did our best to calm them down. I told the family to be quiet because there were other patients who were very sick who needed their rest. The daughter told me that if I didn't "shut my piehole" she would put me in the EYE-CEE-YOUUU.

She then turned on her brother and gave him a straight-out punch to the nose, crying out that he was going to "kill mama." The brother then took a swing at his sister and the two of them fell on mama's bed. We immediately paged Dr. Sweet to the ICU. Within a few moments, Dr. Sweet (which actually consisted of three security guards) arrived to take the loving family away and let mama go.

—Dr. Anita, Oakland, California

I'll Do the Buffet

It was about 4:30 P.M. in the afternoon when a Korean man was admitted to the ER with self-inflicted pen wounds. During a flight from Korea to San Francisco, this guy decided to gouge himself multiple times with a pen. Upon landing, he was taken by security to an ambulance and transported to us. He was evaluated in the ER and sent to the psych ward for additional evaluation.

I went down to get something to eat on the third-floor patio. While I was having dinner, I heard a crash and then this Korean guy landed on the table next to me and went splat. He had broken the window in his room on the eighth floor and took a swan dive into the buffet. I didn't even get my dessert.

—**Dr. Anita, Oakland, California**

You've Got to Have Heart

A man was brought by helicopter to the LAC-USC County emergency room after having sustained a shotgun blast to the left chest. On arrival, he had a pulse of 70 bpm (beats per minute) but no recordable blood pressure. The trauma chief resident performed an ER resuscitative thoracotomy (surgical incision to the chest). Once he opened the chest, he paused, looked around, and seemed confused.

Between the nurses, ER doctors, surgeons, ER techs, and medical students, there must have been about ten people standing around the gurney waiting for this guy to do something. The trauma surgeon attending was standing behind the chief resident, and saw him pause. His face reddened and he got angry at him for not proceeding quickly. Then he yelled, "What the hell are you doing? Hurry up and clamp the aorta." The resident replied, "I don't see the heart." The attending surgeon then stepped up to the patient and realized the heart had been completely destroyed by the gunshot blast. All they could see was pacing wires left over from a pacemaker coming out from the left chest wall.

It turns out that the "heartbeat" detected by the monitors originated from a previously implanted demand double-chamber pacemaker. This was an unsurvivable injury since the heart was no longer present.

—Dr. Cary, Los Angeles, California

MORE MEDICAL
BLOOPERS

The lab test indicated abnormal lover function.

The baby was delivered, the cord clamped and cut and handed to the pediatrician, who breathed and cried immediately.

Exam of genitalia reveals that he is circus sized.

She stated that she had been constipated for most of her life until she got a divorce.

Rectal exam revealed a normal-size thyroid. (Long fingers?)

Between you and me, we ought to be able to get this lady pregnant.

Acronyms

MVA	motor vehicle accident
NFN	normal for Norfolk—possible product of inbreeding
NLPR	no longer playing records (dead)
PBTB	pine box to bedside; indicates an imminent demise
POPTA	passed out prior to arrival
SPAK	status post ass-kicking
TAT	tired all the time
TBC	total body crunch—refers to multiple bone injuries

Having a Hard Head Is Not a Bad Thing

Pereira was shot six times in the head after an altercation with her ex-husband was admitted to the hospital and survived. "I can't explain how this happened," said her doctor, Adriano Teixeira.

The patient was shot in the small city of Monte Claros, about 900 kilometers (560 miles) north of Sao Paulo. She had been quarreling with her former husband, who was reportedly upset because she refused to get back together with him. She was also shot once in the hand.

Doctors could not explain why the .32-caliber bullets did not penetrate Pereira's skull and didn't even need to be extracted immediately. The bullets were lodged just underneath the scalp. She was released and is doing well.

—Various news sources

Nice Hair

A nurse was on duty in the emergency room, when a young woman with purple hair styled into a punk rocker Mohawk, sporting a variety of tattoos, and wearing strange clothing entered. It was quickly determined that the patient had acute appendicitis, so she was scheduled for immediate surgery. When she was completely disrobed on the operating table, the staff noticed that her pubic hair had been dyed green, and above it there was a tattoo that read, "Keep off the grass." Once the surgery was completed, the surgeon wrote a short note on the patient's dressing, which said, "Sorry, had to mow the lawn."

—Retold from various sources

Don't Forget the Keys

A middle-aged man presented himself to the ER with abdominal pains. He told us he swallowed his house keys after an argument with his recently divorced wife. The wife claimed that she was entitled to the house and the patient swallowed the keys after putting special security locks on the door—that could only be opened or changed with the original keys.

The patient was told that it was imperative that they operate but he refused and left.

The follow-up on this is there was a court order demanding that he hand over the keys to his wife, but authorities were not sure how to enforce it.

—From various news sources

Burrito Supreme

A forty-five-year-old man with a history of schizophrenia was brought to the ER with abdominal pain and constipation. A clinical diagnosis of a bowel obstruction was made. A CT scan of the abdomen revealed a complete obstruction at the ileocecal valve (the transition point between the small bowel and the start of the colon).

The surgery team talked to the family and patient, and the number-one possibility was an obstructing cancer. There were close to twenty family members in the ER and most of them were now hysterical and even combative. (One of them fainted and had to be admitted to the hospital with a closed head injury.)

The patient was transferred to the OR (operating room) for an abdominal exploration. Once in the abdomen, the area of obstruction was identified but the "mass" appeared to be freely mobile. An incision was made onto the small bowel (enterotomy) and a large white, slimy mass was removed. The "specimen" was opened on a back table. This "potential tumor" turned out to be a 10 x 10-inch piece of paper, aluminum on one side and on the other side it read "Taco Bell, Burrito Supreme."

—Dr. Erick, northern California

Tug-of-War

A nursing supervisor told me this story the other night. We had a man who was recovering from surgery. Oftentimes the pain medications restrict urine flow and we insert a Foley catheter into the patient's penis. This is done to extract the urine that flows into a plastic bag. When the bag is full, the nurse will remove it and attach a new bag.

Well, this man for some reason went to the toilet and dropped the urine bag into the toilet and then flushed. He let out a horrible HOWL. When the nurse came into the room, the man was having a tug-of-war with the toilet on one side and the catheter that was still attached on the other.

—Dr. J.B., Ann Arbor, Michigan

Good for Fishing

A fifty-year-old woman presented with intermittent, crampy pain in the right lower quadrant of the abdomen. The pain had started after a trip to Europe. She had no obvious signs of distress. No vomiting, diarrhea, or changes in her bowel habits. Upon physical examination, she only had mild tenderness. All blood tests were normal. A radiograph (X-ray) was normal. A colonoscopy was ordered and revealed something quite startling. The patient's abdomen was consumed with worms of at least 1 centimeter— and they were crawling all over the place.

—Anonymous

A Big One

A woman presented herself to the hospital having severe abdominal pain. She appeared to be pregnant, but surgeons in the town of Gospic, Croatia, removed a twenty-two pound tumor from the female patient.

Doctors were shocked when she appeared in the hospital with abdominal pain. Upon examination, they found that the tumor had virtually filled her entire abdominal cavity.

—From various news sources

Stone Cold Hurt

In the Somdej Phraupharajthabo Hospital in Nong Khai province northeast of Bangkok, Dr. Wattana Parisri removed 421 kidney stones from a sixty–year-old woman.

After complaining of abdominal pain, the woman presented herself to the hospital. Initially, she was diagnosed with ulcers but on closer examination, kidney stones were discovered. It is thought to be a record, although kidney stones are a common complaint in northeast Thailand.

—From various news sources

A survey of six countries has revealed that the United States has the worst rate of medical errors.

The Commonwealth Fund's International Health Policy Survey of Sicker Adults compared the experiences of patients in six countries (Australia, Canada, Germany, New Zealand, the United Kingdom and the United States).

Medical Slang

Tough stick—a patient that it is difficult to draw blood from

Train wreck—when a patient has multiple medical problems and complications that will keep the doctor up all night

Trauma handshake—This is a digital rectal exam, which is often traumatic to the patient.

Treat and street—to treat a patient in the ER or clinic without admitting them to the hospital

Turf—when a patient is transferred to another service

Two dudes—This is always the answer when doctors ask a patient who beat them up, as in "I was walking down the street minding my own business when these two dudes jumped me for no reason." The implication is that if it were only one dude the patient would have won the fight.

Virgin abdomen—definition for a patient that has never had abdominal surgery

Wall—a physician (usually a resident) adept at preventing admissions to his service

Yahtzee—term used when all of your patients have been discharged

And Baby Makes Two?

At Pakistan's Institute of Medical Sciences in Islamabad, doctors removed two fetuses, one of them fully grown from the abdomen of a forty-five-day-old baby.

"Such cases are very rare," said Dr. Muqqadar Shah.

Doctors carried out the surgery after X-rays and ultrasound tests showed abnormal growth in the abdomen. The doctors were surprised to discover a fully grown fetus weighing 2.2 pounds.

The mother actually had triplets, but the other two grew inside the baby's abdomen.

—From various news sources

Nail 'Em

In Oregon, a thirty-three-year-old man presented himself to the ER at OHSU, the Oregon Health and Science University Hospital, complaining of dizziness and a headache. It was discovered that the man had botched a suicide attempt and shot twelve nails into his head.

Six of the nails were clustered between his right eye and ear. The heads of the nail caught on the skull and the points entered his brain. The remaining nails were shot around the rest of his face and head. He walked around like this for a day before going to the hospital.

Doctors had to peel back his face and remove the nails with pliers and a drill. He was given antibiotics, a tetanus shot, and psychiatric care. Twenty-five days later he walked out of the hospital.

—Various news sources

A Tall Tail

Doctors saw a man in Alipurduar in West Bengal because he had a thirteen-inch tail. Thousands worshiped this man from India who loved climbing trees and eating bananas. Doctors have offered to remove the tail surgically but the man, Chandre Oram, has refused, stating that it is part of him.

—From several news sources

Don't Stick Out Your Tongue, Young Man

A condition known as hypertrophy (enlargement of muscles) can sometimes be seen with the tongue. The size of the tongue can reach such extremes that it becomes too large for the mouth and rolls over the chin, reaching down as far as the chest. It may even cause the sufferer to choke on his or her own tongue.

Don't Shake My Hand, Please

A young truck driver arrived at the Rehabilitation Center in Valencia, Spain, in 2004 with an amputation of the left arm two inches above the elbow.

The twenty-five-year-old had his arm severed off in a tragic accident. When he appeared in the hospital, surgeons worked tirelessly to reattach the arm, but because the arm had fallen into a drainage pit before being found, a terrible infection ensued.

The doctors, therefore, reattached the limb to his groin where it was kept alive—by feeding it with blood through its veins and arteries. Meanwhile, doctors worked to cure the infection on the upper portion of the left arm.

The patient lived with his arm attached to his groin for nine days until the wound was clean and doctors reimplanted the arm in its original place.

Doctors from the hand and reconstructive surgery department reconstructed bone, arteries, veins, nerves, muscles, and skin in a procedure that lasted six hours.

—From news sources and journals

Fly the Friendly Skies

A thirty-seven-year-old man was shot in the abdomen in India, his country of origin. He spent a few days at home without much relief. However, when his fever increased and his nausea worsened, he booked a plane ticket to the United States—where he was sure his relatives would help him get medical attention.

On the flight he noticed a sudden "release" of feculent purulent material out of his left midback. (*Feculent* refers to the smell of feces, and *purulent* refers to pus.) Nearby passengers started to complain about the smell and soon it became an environmental issue.

The man arrived at the hospital's ER, and after being evaluated by the surgery team, he underwent a left colectomy with end colostomy. After being shot in the abdomen, he apparently developed a localized, initially well-contained abscess. Stool continued to leak into the abscess cavity, so that when the pressure was high enough during the flight, the abscess decompressed through the left retroperitoneum, and out his left midback, creating a "peritoneo-cutaneous fistula." (*Peritoneo* refers to the peritoneal cavity; *cutaneous* refers to skin; *fistula* is an abnormal tubelike passage between two spaces.) This may have prevented him from becoming septic and dying, by draining the infected material out of his body, almost like a natural, self-induced colostomy. He eventually did well and was discharged from the hospital.

In the final analysis, the man's own body blew a hole out of his back when the pressure changed on his flight and his feces dripped from his back while on the plane. The doctors operated and he did well.

—Dr. M., Van Nuys, California

Acronyms

TDS	terminal deceleration syndrome—this refers to death as a result of a sudden stop, such as falling to one's death
TEETH	tried everything else, try homeopathy
TTR	tooth-to-tattoo ratio, also known as a dirt bag
TUBE	totally unnecessary breast exam
UBI	unexplained beer injury
UPF	unpassed fart, describing gaseous distention as seen on an X-ray of the abdomen
VD	veak and dizzy—This is often seen with older people who just don't feel "right." There is usually no specific complaint, but he/she decided something must be wrong. For some reason, it usually occurs in the ER in the middle of the night. "I am just weak and dizzy."

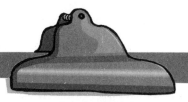

IT'S HOW YOU
WANT TO LOOK AT IT

✓ According to the Center for Health Administration, one out of every ten Americans spends one day a year in the hospital.

✓ A typical surgical skin graft is done with a slice of skin eight thousandths of an inch thick.

✓ In ancient China, doctors were forbidden to see their female patients naked. This posed a severe problem for them and an impossible situation when trying to diagnose a patient. To alleviate this problem doctors on house calls brought with them a small ivory carving of a woman's naked body, which was then passed into the curtained bedchamber of the ailing woman. The patient was instructed to mark the troubled areas where she was having pain or distress. The carving was then passed back through the curtains to the doctor, who made his diagnosis based on the markings made by the patient.

The Doorknob Guy

There have been so many great stories, but this is one I'll never forget. This guy comes into the ER with stomach pain and can't really tell us what he thinks is causing it. We take him down to X-ray and there it is, clear as daylight—a doorknob complete with the assembly smack in the middle of his colon. On an X-ray everything that is solid shows up white, and this was as white as a piece of chalk.

We wheeled the patient into one of the gynecology rooms and had him wait for the doctor. (This was the surgeon who had operated on this guy recently.) The patient had been released only two weeks prior with a colostomy after having an eight ball removed from his colon. The surgeon was an older man, very conservative and well mannered. He entered the room, greeted the man, and looked at the X-ray.

The patient was put into stirrups and we proceeded to use a speculum and forceps to remove the doorknob by grabbing the assembly and just guiding it out. I remember it made a distinct "pop" when it came out.

The doctor removed his gloves and as he was leaving the room turned to the patient and said, "Get a new boyfriend."

—Jordan, RN, Manhattan Beach, California

Stash the Cash

A bag lady came into the ER with a horrible urinary tract infection. Upon examination, we found that she had been stashing money up her vagina. The head nurse said, "Honey, it's not a bank!" She replied, "I only keep the tens and twenties there."

—Jordan, RN, Manhattan Beach, California

That's a Real Problem

A young woman was rushed to the ER with hives all over her body. She was wheezing, itching, and her breathing was labored. She was complaining of chest tightness and felt that she was burning up.

After a physician examined the patient, her boyfriend admitted that they had had sex for the very first time that night and it was shortly thereafter that the symptoms presented themselves.

We were pretty sure what it was after we ruled out any serious problems but called in a gynecologist just to make sure.

The woman had human seminal plasma hypersensitivity, which means that she was allergic to her boyfriend's semen.

Left untreated, this is a sure relationship killer. We wondered if the couple ever had another date.

—Anonymous

Undercover

You see all kinds of people in the ER. One night a very loud drunk showed up with some bruises after falling down—after standing up. During the evaluation, he announced to the entire team that he was a secret agent working for the CIA. The trauma chief leaned down to the patient and quietly said, "Aren't you supposed to keep that information secret?" The patient replied, "Oh yeah!"

—Sarah, RN, Ohio

Not Now, Stanley

A patient who was brought into the ER was not responding to anything we did to wake her up. We pinched her, performed sternal rubs, poked her with needles to start IVs, and hooked her up to monitors. Nothing we did worked and she still would not open her eyes, moan, or show any signs that she would awaken.

We were going to incubate her to protect her airway when the attending physician asked for a rectal temperature. Everyone in the room rolled their eyes, because we knew it would not have changed our care. Besides, the patient didn't feel hot. But we did it anyway and were proven wrong. As the rectal temperature probe was placed in the patient's rectum, she grimaced, waved her hand in the general area of her bottom, and stated in a clear strong voice, "Not now, Stanley!" The probe was taken out and the patient went back to her very deep sleep.

—Anonymous

Airborne

A young eighteen-year-old man came in to the trauma bay after being thrown off the roof of the car he was hanging onto that was being driven by his buddy. After the driver was finally able to stop, he ran over to the young man. The patient was OK but needed to go to the operating room to have his leg fixed. Right before the patient was taken to the OR the trauma chief looked at the patient and asked, "I am curious . . . when did you realize that things were going terribly wrong?" The patient blushed and stated, "When I realized I was airborne." The patient's father was in the room and started to laugh uncontrollably. The laughter was infectious and the patient was taken to the OR by a group of people laughing so hard they were crying.

—Anonymous

Humpty-dumpty doctor—a physiatrist or rehabilitation physician who has to put the pieces back together after a mental breakdown or accident

Knuckledragger—orthopedist

Pecker checker—urologist

Pediatron—pediatrician

Rear admiral—proctologist

Short-order chef—morgue worker

Slasher—surgeon

Stream team—the urology service collectively

MORE MEDICAL
BLOOPERS

The patient lives at home with his mother, father, and pet turtle, who is presently enrolled in day care three times a week.

Both breasts are equal and reactive to light and accommodation.

Exam of genitalia was completely negative except for the right foot.

The patient was to have a bowel resection. However, he took a job as a stockbroker instead.

Examination reveals a well-developed male lying in bed with his family in no distress.

Not My Kind of Party

Several years ago the residents used to have parties on the roof of the hospital during the summer to celebrate the graduating residents and to welcome the incoming residents. These parties were often quite wild. A few years back there was an especially obnoxious new resident who drank so much tequila he passed out.

A few of the older residents, accompanied by some of the incoming doctors, wheeled their inebriated colleague to the cast room where he was dressed in a full-body cast, head to toe with a Foley catheter inserted into his penis.

A few hours later, the young resident woke up with a horrible headache. That was not the least of his problems when he realized he couldn't move. Everyone had quite a laugh about this. Shortly thereafter, administrators at the hospital put an end to the resident parties.

—Anonymous

Happy to Be with You

One evening, a patient who was clearly inebriated with a couple of lacerations to his head was brought into the ER. As we began to stitch him up, the nurse realized he had a full erection. She thought he had a neurological condition and asked if we should send him for a CT. The attending physician calmly put his arm around the nurse who was concerned and said, "He is not only OK, he is very happy to be here with you."

—Anonymous

Yuck and Double Yuck

During an operation, any organ or tissue becomes a "specimen" that is handled by pathology to generate a "final histologic diagnosis." Normally, these specimens are placed in formalin to be preserved until properly studied.

After an urgent left colectomy for an obstructing colon cancer in which both ends of the segment to be taken out are stapled, the specimen was placed in a large bucket of formalin (a colorless solution of formaldehyde) and sent to pathology on a Friday afternoon. The specimen sat in pathology over the weekend.

On Monday, when one of the lab technicians was about to handle the "specimen" for sectioning, she lifted the lid and the colon exploded, releasing a large amount of gas and stool onto her face, into her hair, and all over her clothes.

The formalin had not come in contact with the lumen (inside of the colon) because of the staples on both ends, so bacteria continued to metabolize material inside the colon over the weekend, thereby releasing gas. The pressure eventually disrupted the tissue and the gas and stool followed the path of least resistance onto the technician's face. Because of the emotional trauma, she no longer works in pathology.

Consequently, the new policy is that someone from the surgical team has to "cut open" every specimen, whether it is resected for benign disease or malignancy, before it is sent to pathology.

—Dr. Cara, Van Nuys, California

Style Setter

We work long hours and often are very tired. One night, an ER physician who had not had enough sleep came in to work on a night shift wearing his sweatshirt inside out, food stains on his Batman pajama bottoms, and fuzzy slippers. The poor guy's alarm clock went off and he rushed to work without realizing that he had not changed clothes. We could do something about the sweatshirt and the pj's but he spent the entire night wearing fuzzy slippers.

—Margaret, RN, San Francisco, California

Positive Cheeto Sign

Oftentimes when parents rush into the emergency room believing their child's stomachache is life threatening, we take a look at the child and see that his/her hands are marked with orange. This is the sign that tells us the kid stuffed himself on Cheetos and it isn't an emergency, says Jordan Weiss, a registered nurse in Los Angeles.

Medical School

I still think the funniest thing happened when I was a first-year medical student. We were in gross anatomy and I'll never forget Myra, otherwise known as Iron Pants. She was mean, tough, and hated men. Most of all she thought she was God's gift to medicine and thought she was better than the rest of us. She made our lives miserable, but when it came time to dissect the male genitalia, we had a plan.

We figured Myra had never actually seen a man undressed, but as always, she insisted on doing the dissections while we held the charts. My buddy came up with a plan to get back at her for the torture she had put us through, but it would take a little work to get it done.

The three of us went into the lab at night and went to work on our cadaver in preparation for class and Myra the next morning.

We inserted a small rubber tube into the penis of the cadaver. The tube was connected to a rubber ball that when squeezed would inflate the penis.

When morning came, we were the first ones there, which should have been a clue to Myra because we were never on time.

As usual, Myra insisted on doing the physical work, which today we were more than happy to oblige. She placed her knife at the base of the penis and gingerly held the organ, stretching the skin upward so that she could make the incision.

My hand was in my pocket on the squeeze ball ready to inflate the tubing simultaneously with the first nick of the knife. Just as Myra touched the penis as if in a sudden burst of male outrage, the penis suddenly came alive. It stiffened, and a liquid stream burst from it, straight into the shocked and unbelieving face of its tormenter. The entire class was in hysterics as Myra stomped out of class. We of course were called into the deans' office and were put on probation, but it was well worth it.

—Dr. George, Ann Arbor, Michigan

The Eyes Have It

A thirty-five-year-old man entered the ER complaining of eye pain and blurry vision. Upon examination, it was discovered that the man had not changed his contact lenses for over a year. The lenses fused into his eyes and he was using a second set of contacts to correct the vision from the first pair. When his eyesight still didn't improve, he bought disposable contact lenses and used those over the first two pairs. By the next day, his eyes had reacted badly. He now had three pairs of contact lenses in his eyes and it was only then that he sought medical attention.

—China

"They Certainly Give Strange Names to Diseases"

—Plato, Greek author and philosopher (428 BC–347 BC)

Air Controllers Syndrome: Peptic ulcers frequently occur among air traffic controllers, one of the most stressful jobs. (*ILLINOIS MEDICAL JOURNAL*, 1972)

Alice In Wonderland Syndrome: Also called micropsia, this condition distorts visual perception so that objects that are close appear disproportionately tiny, as though viewed through the wrong end of a telescope. Named after Lewis Carroll's Alice from *Alice's Adventures in Wonderland*. Carrol suffered migraines, which is often a cause of this syndrome.

Alopecia Walkmania: This is loss of hair from prolonged use of personal stereo headphones. (*JOURNAL OF THE AMERICAN MEDICAL ASSOCIATION*, 1984) NOTE: TECHNOLOGICAL IMPROVEMENTS LIKE EARBUDS HAVE NO DOUBT REDUCED RATES OF THIS AILMENT.

Beer Drinker's Finger: Hey, dude, this is a swelling, and/or a bluish discoloration caused by placing pop-top beer can rings on a finger. (*JAMA*, 1968)

Bingo Brain: This headache is associated with carbon monoxide intoxication that occurs after spending long hours in smoke-filled bingo halls. (*CANADIAN MEDICAL ASSOCIATION*, 1982)

Birdwatchers' Twitch: This is the nervous excitement or twitch after spotting a species for the first time. (*NEW SCIENTIST*, 1982)

Body Builders' Psychosis: These psychotic episodes, associated with the use of anabolic steroids, can cause hallucinations, paranoid delusions, grandiose beliefs, and manic-depressive symptoms. (*LANCET*, 1987)

Booksellers' Bends: This is a sickness that is caused by changes in atmospheric pressure—for example, when a customer or bookseller climbs a ladder in a bookstore and feels sick.

Casino Feet: This is soreness that occurs on the feet after long hours standing in front of slot machines. (*WILMINGTON MORNING STAR*, 1981)

Cat Scratch Fever: This is an infectious disease usually found in children one to two weeks after a scratch.

Chicken Neck: This is a partial dislocation and arthritis of the joint of the middle finger from continued use of this finger to dislocate chicken necks for slaughtering. (*BMA JOURNAL*, 1955)

Christmas Depression: This relatively common ailment is caused by psychological stress during holidays related to the use of alcohol and social pressures. (*JAMA*, 1982)

Credit-Card-itis: This is pain in the rear that runs down the thigh due to pressure on a nerve from a wallet stuffed with credit cards. (*NEW ENGLAND MEDICAL JOURNAL*, 1966)

Disco Digit: Dance the night away and you'll get a sore finger from snapping fingers while dancing. (*NEW ENGLAND MEDICAL JOURNAL*)

Dog Walkers' Elbow: Go–dog–go! This is the pain caused by constant tension and tugs from a dog leash. (NEW ENGLAND MEDICAL JOURNAL, 1979)

Electrical Sensitivity: Condition when a person reports physical or psychological sensitivity from devices like cell phones, wifi, and other electrical devices. (*UK HEALTH PROTECTION AGENCY*)

Electronic Space-War Video-game Epilepsy: If you see your kid flapping around on the floor, it might be a kind of epilepsy caused by the flashing lights of electronic video games. (*BMA JOURNAL*, 1982)

Espresso Wrist: This is wrist pain in espresso coffee-machine operators from strong wrist motions required in making the coffee. It was reported in the *Journal of the American Medical Association* in 1956, and no doubt is much worse now when there is a coffee bar on almost every corner. (*JAMA,* 1956)

Flip-flop Dermatitis: This is a skin disease that occurs on the feet from wearing rubber flip-flops. (*BMA Journal,* 1965)

Foreign Language Syndrome: This is when someone awakens from an injury speaking with a foreign accent even though they have never visited or lived in the country where the accent is from.

Frisbee Finger: This is a cut on the finger due to strenuous throwing of a Frisbee. (*New England Medical Journal,* 1975)

Golf Arm: This is a cousin to tennis elbow, but nevertheless a real ailment. It is shoulder and elbow pain after too many rounds of golf. (*BMA Journal,* 1896)

Hooker's Elbow: This is painful shoulder swelling suffered by fishermen from repeatedly jerking upward on a fishing line. (*New England Medical Journal,* 1981) (Not to be confused with a technique used in various brothels.)

Houswifitis: These are nervous symptoms related to spending too much time managing a busy household. (*Centrescope,* 1976)

Humpers Lump: This is swelling suffered by hotel porters from lugging heavy bags. (*Diseases of Occupations,* 1975)

Ice-cream Frostbite: This is frostbite on the lips from prolonged contact with ice cream. (*New England Medical Journal,* 1982)

Jazz Ballet Bottom: These are painful abscesses suffered by dancers who frequently spin on their bottoms. (*Daily Telegraph,* 1987)

Jean Folliculitis: This is irritation of the hair follicles from the waist down to the knees caused by ultratight jeans. This probably was big in the seventies and is now making a comeback. (*New England Medical Journal,* 1981)

Joystick Digit: This is a pain in the trigger finger due to prolonged use of video-game joysticks. (*JAMA,* 1987)

Knife Sharpener's Cramp: This is painful hand swelling from sharpening too many knives. (*Diseases of Occupations*, 1975)

Label Licker's Tongue: Ulcers form in the mouth after licking sticky labels. (*Dangerous Trades*, 1902)

Maple Syrup Urine Disease: This is a genetic disease that causes urine to smell like maple syrup. (National Institutes of Health)

Money Counter's Cramp: This is a painful seizure of muscles from counting too much cash. (*English University Press*, 1975)

Motorway Blues: This type of headache has been noted by drivers on congested motorways. (*BMA Journal*, 1963)

Nun's Knee: This is a painful swelling of the kneecap from repeated kneeling in prayer. (*Diseases of Occupations*, 1975)

Ondine's Curse: A sleep disorder resulting from a malfunctioning autonomic nervous system. Its victims are unable to breathe on their own but must consciously will each and every breath. They will suffocate if they fall asleep. Respirators may help.

Ondine's Curse gets its name from the legend of a water nymph, Ondine, who fell in love with a human, therby forfeiting her immortality. Though he had pledged his undying love, Ondine discovered him snoring in the arms of another woman. She cursed him and kicked her husband awake, pointed her finger at him, and uttered her curse: "You swore faithfulness to me with every waking breath, and I accepted your oath. So be it. As long as you are awake, you shall have your breath, but should you ever fall asleep, then that breath will be taken from you and you will die!"

Oyster Shucker's Keratitis: This is eye irritation that occurs from contact with fragments of oyster shells. (*BMA Journal*, 1896)

Panty Girdle Syndrome: This is a tingling or swelling of feet from wearing a too-tight panty girdle. (*BMA Journal*, 1972)

Player's Liver: This is the hazard of spending too long in the bar instead of playing the game. (*Encyclopedia of Sports*, 1971)

Quick-draw Leg: This is a bullet wound in the leg from practicing fast draw from a gun in a belt holster. (*JAMA*, 1966)

Reflex Horn Syndrome: This is the tendency for drivers waiting in traffic jams to toot horns. (*NEW ENGLAND MEDICAL JOURNAL*, 1976)

Retired Husband Syndrome: This is the tension, headaches, depression, and anxiety that is felt by women whose husbands have just retired. (*WESTERN JOURNAL OF MEDICINE*, 1984)

Seamstresses' Bottom: This is the hardening of skin following long-term trauma of rocking on the hips while operating a sewing machine. (*AMERICAN FAMILY PHYSICIAN*, 1979)

Sick Santa's Syndrome: This is lower back pain from lifting heavy children and parcels—acquired illnesses from multiple contact with kids. (*JAMA*, 1986)

Television Legs: This is loss of normal flexibility of the legs from being slumped in a chair in front of the box for too long. (*JAMA*, 1958)

Toilet Seat Dermatitis: This is skin irritation on the rear from spending too much time on the toilet. (*ARCHIVE OF DERMATOLOGY*, 1933)

Uniform Rash: This is skin irritation of the neck, chest, and arms from wearing new uniforms. (*BMJ*, 1973)

Volkswagen Dermatitis: This is an allergic skin reaction caused by rubber bumper guards. (*ARCHIVE OF DERMATOLOGY*, 1971)

Wiiitis: pronounced "wee-eye-tis." This is the latest ailment to develop from video games, starting with the 1981 condition Space Invaders' wrist, which was caused by the repeated button-pushing required by the popular arcade game. Wiiitis has now been seen in a number of patients who play tennis with the new Nintendo video console Wii.

Working Wife Syndrome: This is fatigue, irritability, headaches, and diminished sex drive encountered from the strain of doing two jobs. (*LANCET*, 1966)

Yoga Foot Drop: This is paralysis of the foot due to compounded pressure from practicing yoga positions. (*JAMA*, 1971)

Man Burns Genitals
in *Jackass* Stunt

Attempts to replicate a movie stunt landed one man in the ER with burned genitals and another facing criminal charges. The men were trying to do a stunt from one of the *Jackass* movies, in which a character lights his genitals on fire.

A young man suffered serious burns to his hands and genitals, according to the criminal complaint after his "friend" sprayed lighter fluid on him, setting him on fire. The friend was charged with felony battery and first-degree reckless endangerment.

The young man pulled down his pants and let his friend spray him with lighter fluid. When the fire didn't catch, more lighter fluid was splashed on. WHOOSH! The fire ignited, setting the young man's genitals, hands, and clothes on fire.

He ran into the bathroom, jumped into the tub, and put the flames out. A short time later, he was taken to the Regions Hospital Burn Unit in St. Paul, Minnesota, for second-degree burns.

He told police that he didn't want anyone to get in trouble because of the stunt.

The friend was freed on bond. If convicted, he faces up to ten years in prison.

—Eau Claire, Wisconsin

MORE MEDICAL
BLOOPERS

The patient experienced sudden onset of severe shortness of breath with a picture of acute pulmonary edema at home while having sex that gradually deteriorated in the emergency room.

The patient is an eighty-nine-year-old widow who no longer lives with her husband.

Many years ago the patient had frostbite of the right shoe.

The bugs that grew out of her urine were cultured in the lab and are not available. I WILL FIND THEM!!!

Thank you to all of the doctors, nurses, and hospital personnel who have contributed to this book. A very special thanks to Dr. George Brewer who graciously let us reprint some of the stories from his memoir *From Start to Finish*. Thanks to all of those in cyberspace and the listmakers who have told and retold stories and provided us with great tales. We are sorry we cannot thank everybody. A special thanks to Uwe and Kate for believing in this book; Bethy for taking an early read; J.B. for her insight; Nikki, Erica, Ellie, and Monica for listening to these stories over dinner; and, of course, the doctors, nurses, and techs who despite the funny stories are out there every day saving lives.

Did They Really Say That? Medical Records quotes were taken from actual medical records dictated by physicians. They appeared in a column written by Richard Lederer, PhD. The authors wish to thank Dr. Lederer for letting us reprint his work.

ACKNOWLEDGMENTS